Inside Out Families

Inside Out Families
Living the Faith Together

Diana Garland

BAYLOR UNIVERSITY PRESS

Unless otherwise stated, scripture quotations are from the New Revised Standard Version Bible, copyright 1989, Division of Christian Education of the National Council of the Churches of Christ in the United States of America. Used by permission. All rights reserved.

Cover design by Andrew Brozyna, AJB Design, Inc.

Library of Congress Cataloging-in-Publication Data

Garland, Diana S. Richmond, 1950-
  Inside out families : living the faith together / Diana Garland.
      p. cm.
  Includes bibliographical references and index.
  ISBN 978-1-60258-245-3 (pbk. : alk. paper)
  1. Families--Religious life. 2. Service (Theology) 3. Theology, Practical. I. Title.
  BV4526.3.G365 2009
  253.085--dc22

                                                    2009027656

Printed in the United States of America on acid-free paper with a minimum of 30% pcw recycled content.

To Dennis Myers and Terry Wolfer
My work partners and lifelong friends

Table of Contents

Acknowledgments

My profound appreciation goes to the families who gave so freely of their time, a scarce commodity in family life today, particularly for these families that are deeply engaged in serving their communities as well as working jobs and caring for one another. I wish it were possible for me to identify them all by name; they are the unsung heroes that daily weave the fiber of church and community life. As is customary in research such as this, however, I agreed with them that they would remain anonymous so that they could speak candidly. They will, of course, recognize themselves in the stories they told me.

This project developed with the nurture and support of a host of colleagues and friends. I am grateful to Craig Dykstra and Chris Coble of Lilly Endowment, Inc., for their encouragement, invaluable guidance, and support for this series of projects. Dennis Myers, Terry Wolfer, David Sherwood, Beryl Hugen, and Paula Sheridan were my colleagues in the Service and Faith Project. We traveled to intensive work retreats together in various places across the country, and in between, we spent countless hours interviewing congregation leaders and members and then on conference calls, hammering out together what we were learning about how service and Christian faith are related to one another. Dennis Myers, Terry Wolfer, and I continued on in this project for what has become a decade of working together, digging through hundreds of pages of transcripted interviews, and becoming lifelong friends in the process. Early on, the scope of this project was enhanced by great consultants: Dan Aleshire, Courtney Bender, Fred DeJong, Robert Franklin, Edwin Hernandez, Bill Lockhart, Gene Roehlkepartain, Christopher Smith, Heidi Unruh, and Gaynor Yancey. Scott Taylor, Michael Sherr, and Kelly Atkinson were graduate students who worked diligently with the project in its various phases.

Once I had crafted the first draft of this book, I shared it with several of the families whose stories I have told. They gave generous feedback, corrected me where I needed it, and confirmed that I have understood the stories they shared with us. One family took the manuscript on a beach vacation together, and read excerpts out loud for family discussion. I cannot think of any use of this book that could bring me more satisfaction than as a discussion starter for a family! My colleague Gaynor Yancey and my journalist daughter Sarah Garland edited the entire manuscript and made very helpful suggestions.

Above all, I thank my husband, David Garland, my biblical scholar in residence. David is now Professor of Christian Scriptures and Dean at George W. Truett Theological Seminary and Interim President of Baylor University. We have been ministry partners and family for one another for forty years. What I learned about biblical interpretation, I learned from David. Our past writing together, and our editing of one another's individual writings, has refined my thinking. Often, I cannot remember which thoughts first came from whom. As much as he has contributed to my thoughts, he should not be held responsible for my biblical interpretations and theological musings. I am a social scientist by profession, not a theologian. My discussions of biblical content and theology in this book are my reflections as a believing Christian, shaped in a congregation and community of faith where I have lived and worked out my own understandings of how to put my social scientific self with my faithing self and my own family experiences.

This host of people whose names I have written in gratitude is testimony to God's wisdom that "goodness" comes in not being alone in any task. Although the book cover carries my name, I am only a representative of this host of friends, families, and communities who are living sacred stories that carry us through ordinary days and ordinary lives, connecting us to God. This book is only a beginning attempt to understand faith and service as dimensions of family life. I hope others can build on it. I offer it claiming the promise that God can work toward perfect ends even through "weak" efforts (2 Cor 12:9). Above all, it is my prayer that this book will help families together to pour themselves out in service and in so doing, find new life together in Christ.

Introduction

During the years our children were growing up, my husband and I were colleagues in the same seminary, where I taught church social work and David taught New Testament. Our children's growing-up years were therefore spent in a family steeped in seminary life and in the church. Church involvement was never optional for Sarah and John; they had to go with us. When Sarah was fourteen, however, she decided that church was not where she wanted to be on Sunday morning. I kept making her go with us, but she was not happy with me, and I felt fairly certain that forced church attendance was not really going to contribute to a vibrant faith-life for her. I began to cast about for what I could do that would help her live her faith on her own terms.

Our children have always cared deeply about other people, especially about people who live on the margins of society. As a young teen, Sarah cared deeply for all God's creatures, in fact—not just the human variety. About the time Sarah protested going to church, she also became a vegetarian, not because she was concerned about fat and cholesterol in her diet, but because she believed adamantly in animal rights. She also was a strong environmentalist and was concerned about the devastation of the rain forests. That was the teenager I faced off with each Sunday morning: a young woman who never saw an injustice—human, animal, or plant—she did not want to tackle.

How could I involve Sarah in living her faith in a way that made sense to her? If being forced to sit in Sunday worship services was not meaningful to her, then perhaps serving others in a tangible expression of our faith would. One of the graduates of our social work school, Angela, was the executive director of the local shelter for homeless families. I knew that the shelter had a volunteer program, so I called Angela to ask her if we could volunteer with our children. They had never had a family volunteer before, but Angela said "Why not?" Everyone in our family agreed to try it, in itself a signature moment for us during that phase. Our family went through the volunteer training together and was assigned as a "mentor family" to a young family in the shelter, a mother and father and their two elementary-age children, both younger than my children. They had lived in tents and trailers and under bridges for much of the children's lives, following construction work or whatever employment the dad could find to feed his children. Both of the children were behind in school because they had moved so much. The little boy was failing because he had significant hearing loss from an untreated chronic ear infection—they had no medical insurance. He could not hear well in school and had not learned to read.

We began visiting the family while they lived in a tiny apartment at the shelter. Soon, the staff of the shelter helped them secure a permanent home, a very modest cinder block three-room house for rent in the opposite corner of the county from where we lived. For a year, we drove the forty-five minutes each way to visit "our family." Sarah and John helped the children with their homework and their reading skills. David and I visited with the parents and did our best to help them with the various struggles of making it from one day to the next. We did not feel like mentors at all; "mentor" implies that we had something to teach or had great advice to give. In fact, we learned so much from those parents, because they had survival skills we had never had reason to develop. We were simply friends, offering ourselves to one another. We often brought a half gallon of ice cream to share together. John, age eleven, brought the little boy one of his baseball gloves John claimed he had outgrown and taught the little boy to throw a baseball after they finished his reading homework. Sometimes I was able to help the parents navigate the free health clinic, or figure out how to get to work when their old car stopped running. But they really knew much more about free health clinics and the unreliability of public transportation in our county than I did.

On the other hand, what they gave us was more than I could have dreamed. Frankly, I started us on the volunteering path because I wanted to do something to make faith real for my daughter, not out of a burning desire to be a volunteer. Our family's already-crowded hours, with two-career parents, included the usual rounds of children's sporting events, music lessons, church activities, and responsibility for an aging parent. Indeed, the forty-five minutes in the car each way gave us a chance to talk; anyone who knows teenagers knows that the most meaningful conversations between teens and their parents often take place in the car. We talked a lot about the stark differences in the lives and resources of our two families, about what it means to be a Christian in a world where little boys grow up with hearing disabilities because parents cannot get needed health care, a world where mommas and daddies want desperately to support their families but they cannot get to work when their old wreck-of-a-car breaks down and the only affordable housing is miles from the nearest public transportation. Sarah and I were no longer doing battle with one another.[1] We were pondering doing battle with the forces of this world that kept our new friends in poverty and on the brink of homelessness.

Did we help that family? Probably not a lot. The year we had committed to one another ended. We agreed that we wanted to continue to be friends, and we did for a while. But then we moved away for a year's assignment overseas, and when we came back, they had moved on to find better work opportunities in another state. They wrote for a while, but writing was not easy for them; the parents themselves were barely literate. The struggles they faced were so challenging that what we could do to help seemed so small. But we did what we could; we gave our friendship and tried to be faithful to show up each week and care—and in the process, we were changed.

A Framework for Ministry with Families

Lest you give me credit for being a creative mother to come up with the idea of a family service project all on my own in the face of a fourteen-year-old's challenge to make faith relevant in her life, consider the fact that I was teaching family ministry at the time. To teach a subject means having to think deeply about it, so I was thinking a lot about families in the context of faith in those days—and still am seventeen years later. Such thinking is an interesting challenge for me, given my social scientific training. Social scientists study social phenomena to understand them and what causes them. Christian faith is certainly a social phenomenon as it is lived out in the lives of families and communities. To provide leadership for families in the church, however, we need to understand not only what *is* but also what *ought to be*. Understanding families sociologically is helpful, but it is not enough. We also need theological perspectives on family and community life. The social sciences help us know who families are and how they live their lives together. Theology tells us what God intended families to be and how they *ought* to live their lives together. It takes both to lead the church effectively from what we are today to what God is calling us to tomorrow. A framework for family ministry needs to weave these worlds of thought together. Even our definition of family involves seeing through both the lenses of what is (social sciences) and what is ought to be (theology).

Knowing a Family When We See One: Sociological Perspectives

Defining a family would seem to be straightforward; surely we know one when we see one. Unfortunately, our definitions often provide the lens for what we see—and what we do not see. For much of the last century, family sociologists wrestled with what has come to be known as a *structural definition of family* as defined by legal (marriage or adoption) or biological (parent/child) relationships.[2] That is, families are husbands and wives and their children, or what is also called the "nuclear" family. The term "nuclear" refers to the basic unit of family, the "nucleus," not to nuclear energy! In addition, we talk about the "extended" family, or extensions to the "nucleus," consisting of children's grandparents, aunts, uncles, and cousins. That picture of the family—the "traditional family"—has been the norm against which our culture measures other family-like relationships and defines them by how they differ: single-parent families, childless couples, divorced and remarried couples, and never-married adults.

As early as the 1920s, however, sociologists were questioning defining families by these role structures. The influential family sociologist Ernest Burgess suggested that families are better understood when we look not at legal concepts but at how family members interact with one another.[3] Instead of a status to which one is assigned (mother, father, spouse, child) as the primary way of thinking about family, *a functional definition of family* defines the family as those persons who *function* as family for one another. A grandmother may be a distant figure seen once or twice a year on holidays, or she may be the primary parenting figure if the biological mother is drug addicted, mentally ill, or otherwise unavailable to parent. The "grandmother" status is "extended family" when defining the family structurally, but she functions as a mothering figure and so is part of the grandchild's "primary family" using a functional definition.

A functional definition is more sensitive to opportunities for change over time—and for hope. For example, "stepfamilies" is a structural term defining families formed by second marriages with children from first marriages. Whether parents married last week with teenagers, or thirty years ago when their children were infants, the nonbiological parent is still structurally considered a "stepparent." "Blending," on the other hand, is a functional term. "Blending family" recognizes that the family is in an ongoing process of becoming a family together—it was not an action completed when the parents married and became a "stepfamily." "Blending" is a long process of figuring out together how to be family, what the relationships will be today, tomorrow, and in the future.

A functional approach sees a family as the people we stay in communication with even when college or army service or work assignments pull us apart geographically, the people we share our resources—emotional and physical—with, the ones we share our life purposes with, the people we cling to and belong to in the bumps and bruises of life. The families I have interviewed in the studies I will share with you in this book have taught me how important this functional definition of family is when we think about congregational ministry.

When I met her, Ms. Coper was a single mom.[4] For a few months after her son Dan was born, sixteen years before, she had been a welfare recipient, but she used the time she was receiving public support to finish school. She now has a good clerical job and her family lives in a middle-class suburb. They are active members of a large National Baptist church. When I visited them in their home, Ms. Coper was running late coming home, so I had an opportunity for conversation with Dan, who was babysitting four-year-old Joe. Dan introduced Joe as his little brother. In the hour the two of us talked, Dan told me a lot about his family, about his own near-scrapes with trouble and how his mother dragged him to the pastor for fatherly talks about his behavior. She was determined that he would learn self-discipline and to use his strength in positive ways, so she had started him in karate lessons. Joe also told me this about his mother with obvious pride:

> She seems to like working with teenagers a lot. We used to have this youth ministry at church, and we always had teenagers over to the house talking about their problems and stuff. I think it helped some of them out a lot. It really didn't affect me because I always thought that, besides my father being gone, I had the perfect home.

Later, my conversation with Ms. Coper filled out some of what Dan had told me. Joe is in fact Ms. Coper's cousin's baby. Joe's mother is mentally ill, so Ms. Coper is raising Joe as her own son. She is also providing a home, at least temporarily, to a little girl in the neighborhood who will otherwise be placed in a foster home in another area of the city and have to change schools.

Apart from growing up without his father, Dan said that his family is "perfect." He recognized that they did not fit the structural norm of a nuclear family, but he spoke wisdom. Most families these days are not nuclear families, and if we set that structure as the norm, most families by definition can never get there. In defining their family together, Ms. Coper has focused on how they live their life with one another and how they have opened their family to "strangers" who have become part of them. Ms. Coper did not have a huge income; she had to work hard to support Dan. Working and raising a son—and now sons—alone is not easy. Despite the struggles, despite how the world with its structural definition might see them, Dan sees his family as "perfect."

Thinking about What Family Ought to Be for Christians

This functional definition of the family is congruent with a theological understanding of the family based on Jesus' birth, life, and death. In the family tree that opens the Gospel of Matthew, we read fifteen verses of "begats" by one father after another. When it comes to Jesus, however, the pattern changes. Joseph is not named as Jesus' father, because "before they lived together, she was found to be with child from the Holy Spirit" (Matt 1:18). Instead, the writer calls Joseph "the husband of Mary, of whom Jesus was born" (Matt 1:16). Despite the fact that Joseph was not Jesus' biological father, Joseph accepted him as his son by naming him and adopting him as his own (Matt 1:25). The point on which the Gospel writer focuses is not so much the immaculate conception but, instead, the adoption. The conception is a stepping stone to the major point, a reason for why Joseph needed to adopt Jesus.

Later, in his teaching, Jesus uses an incident in his own family to redefine family for his followers. His mother and brothers, concerned for his wellbeing, had heard that his teachings may lead to real trouble and so have come to persuade him to come home and lay low for awhile. They evidently cannot get close enough to him to talk because of the crowd, however, so they send word through the crowd that they are outside and want to speak with him. In response, Jesus says,

> "Who is my mother, and who are my brothers?" And pointing to his disciples, he said, "Here are my mother and my brothers! For

whoever does the will of my Father in heaven is my brother and sister and mother." (Matt 12:48-50)

Jesus teaches, then, that family now means *choosing*—choosing to follow Jesus and thus adopting one another as family. Our shared faith binds us together. We are no longer limited to family relationships defined by biological kinship or marriage (the structural family). In looking at events later in Jesus' life, it becomes clear that Jesus was not severing family ties with his mother and brothers with these words. His mother was with him to the very end of his life, standing at the foot of the cross. His brothers became disciples and leaders in the early church. They *were* family, but they also *became* family to Jesus and to one another—and others—in their choice to follow him.

The Gospel of John records the last teaching of Jesus about family before his death. Mary stood at the foot of the cross with the other women, watching her son suffer. The beloved disciple stood beside her. Jesus looked at her and said, "Woman, here is your son." And to the disciple, he said, "Here is your mother." The very next verse states, "Jesus knew that all was finished" (John 19). Proclaiming this adoptive relationship finished his ministry. This was part of the plan. Would they have cared for one another if Jesus had not spoken them into existence as adoptive family? Perhaps, but clearly, naming the relationship had power. *"And from that hour* the disciple took her to his own home" (John 19:27, emphasis added). They *functioned* as family for one another, despite the absence of biological ties. Perhaps Jesus could have spoken to the group in good Southern idiom, "Y'all take care of one another." But he was not telling the church to be the community of faith in this place; he was turning two people *within* the community into a functional family. They adopted one another.[5]

Ministry with Families

Understanding family from this perspective—as a way we choose and care for one another regardless of the biology and life circumstances we have been dealt—has a profound impact on how we minister with families. A first task of the church is to encourage and nurture the process of adopting one another as family. The nuclear family is no longer the model; Ms. Coper, in fact, is the "perfect" model of Christian family life, seeking out and folding in those who are otherwise alone in this world. Instead of seeing her family as a "single-parent family"—implying not quite whole—her family is truly living the "good news" that in this lonely world, all God's children can be adopted into loving family relationships in the household of God. She is living the first task of family ministry, which is to be sure that no child of God (whether child or adult or older adult) is alone. Everyone needs to belong to a family.

A second task of ministry with families is helping family members live in relationship with one another in ways that point to Jesus' teachings. There is no more effective and challenging crucible for learning to love unconditionally, to be angry and sin not, to confront and to repent, to forgive and be forgiven. Meilaender has called family the "school of virtue" in which God places us, day after day, with persons we are to learn to love.[6] This is the task of ministry with which we are most familiar in congregation leadership today—parent training, marriage education, support groups, and seminars. Ms. Coper's approach to family certainly took into account this dimension of family life. When Dan was flirting with trouble, she tackled the threat head on. She communicated clearly what she expected from him. He perceived that he did not have the problems other teens in his community had because his mother was actively addressing the challenges he and others faced.

The final task, as I have thought about family ministry, is equipping and supporting Christians to use their families as a channel of ministry to others within and outside the community of faith. The first family we read about in the early church is the couple Prisca and Aquila, a very busy family indeed. They instructed others in the faith (Acts 18:26), and they provided a home for those otherwise family-less—like Paul, who lived with them for some time and worked in the family business as a tentmaker (Acts 18:3). Their home was also the church where the Christians met for worship (1 Cor 16:9). Their relationship with one another was the basis for a shared ministry that touched others far beyond themselves. The families of the New Testament were called to open their homes in hospitality to the community of faith and to strangers and to teach the good news to others (Rom 12:13). The focus, then, is not just ministry *to* families, but also ministry *through* families. Ms. Coper and Dan used their family as a channel of ministry to others. They may not have had a church meeting in their home, as did Prisca and Aquila, but they had the church's youth group there, complete with pizza.

Learning from the Families

My premise has been that the goal of family ministry is to empower families to live their faith with one another and in the communities and relationships in which they are embedded. With that goal in mind, I have completed a series of research projects designed to understand what faith looks like in family life, so that we could better accomplish the three tasks of family ministry. The Church Census project was based on whole-congregation surveys focusing on the family life of Christians. Those surveys have been conducted in more than one hundred Protestant congregations in the past fifteen years.[7] Next came the Families and Faith project, which identified the powerful role of family stories and of families serving together in the faith development of children and adults. That project resulted in the book *Sacred Stories of Ordinary Families*.[8]

The findings of the Families and Faith project led to the project that will be the primary focus of this book, called "Service and Faith," a study of Christians who volunteer in various programs of community service through their congregations.[9] The earlier projects really focused on how Christians form families and how they live their daily lives together in ways that express their faith. The Service and Faith project went further to focus on the third task of family ministry—equipping families to serve within and beyond the community of faith. As a part of the larger project, we studied the lives of sixteen families—in a diversity of structures and life stages—who had been engaged in community ministry together for more than a year. The families told inspiring stories of service and faith, extending my understanding of family faith far beyond my previous work. This book shares what those sixteen families taught me, as well as what I learned in the earlier projects that involved more than one hundred families and their congregations.

My understanding of families and their faiths has been significantly altered by what I learned from these families. They are really very "ordinary" families; you will find families like them in every congregation. But when I took the time to learn from them, I came to some startling conclusions. I will give away my conclusion now: the heart of family ministry is equipping families together for a life of Christian service to others beyond themselves, to turn themselves inside out in a calling larger than their own daily life together. As they serve others, they grip a deeper understanding of one another and of God. They find their faith more resilient and meaningful. Their children develop what we call "sticky faith,"[10] a faith that helps them stick to the church and to their beliefs into young adulthood, when their contemporaries are abandoning the church in droves. And adults develop a "sticky faith" that keeps them "stuck" to the church and to God, who carries them through the crises and deep struggles that life inevitably holds.

Now that you know the ending, I hope that the pages that follow will embolden you to focus your attention on ministry *through* families more than ministry *to* families. We will suggest ways to help families and their congregations get started in turning themselves inside out to serve others in the name of Jesus.

Diana Garland
June 1, 2009

1

Families and Faith
Used Furniture, Saws, and Lawn Mowers

When I first met them, Brad and Lisa had just retired. He had spent years on the road as a long-distance trucker. Lisa had been on her feet day after day as a store clerk. Two of their three sons still lived at home. Twenty-four-year-old Tyler worked in a grocery store and Toby, age sixteen, was in high school. Tyler was not home when I visited them, but Toby was there, working a jigsaw puzzle on the coffee table when I arrived. Their oldest son lived nearby with his wife and daughter. Brad is a vivacious, outgoing man, a much-loved deacon in their small Baptist congregation. Lisa, a warm, smiling woman, orchestrated our conversation and cued her son and husband about when to chime in. She was clearly comfortable with using all of her five feet, two inches to control a houseful of men.

I was a stranger in their community, a researcher/professor trying to learn from families in their congregation about how faith gives shape to their daily lives. When their pastor recommended I talk with them, Brad and Lisa had readily agreed, and so here I was. With my tape recorder rolling, I asked them to tell about their life together as a family. As we sipped coffee and talked about their lives, I posed the question, "If I came from another planet and didn't know what the word 'faith' means, how would I understand it from looking at your family?"

Lisa reflected for a moment, and then told me a story about talking her church into helping a family in the community who had lost their home in a three-alarm fire, just five days before the Thanksgiving just past. She had organized the people in her congregation to respond. They brought clothes, appliances, and couches, dropping them off at church and thanking Lisa for her leadership. It was up to Lisa to figure out how to move everything to the rental house where the family was living. The temperature had dropped, and the first snow of the season was falling. So she rented a truck and turned to her three boys and Brad for help. They spent hours moving all she had collected. No one in the family really wanted to spend the snowy evening this way—it was miserably cold and slippery, they all had work to do, friends to hang out with, and the holiday to prepare for. But they did it anyway. Lisa admonished the family by reminding them that God had blessed them and expected them to be a blessing to others.

Toby was listening as his mother told me that story, fingering the puzzle pieces and smiling at the memory. He then joined the conversation by saying that at least three times in a week, he cuts neighbors' lawns. I suppose I looked quizzical about how that fit the conversation about moving furniture on a snowy night, so Lisa explained that he mows grass for women who are single or widowed, and she does not allow them to pay Toby. "I won't let him take any money for it because he needs to do that; he doesn't need the money."

Toby added, "She got me into something else—I have to cut up wood for this lady and she paints it and then we try to sell it." Again, Lisa explained that a woman in their church was disabled and living on a fixed income. She was a skillful painter, however. Toby had received a jigsaw for Christmas, because he likes woodworking. So Lisa had him cutting out shapes that the woman painted, and then Lisa and other women in the church sold them for her, providing her a little extra income. She added, "He's doing pretty well with his woodworking."

Toby laughed, "I get a lot of practice and a lot of exercise with Mom's projects." Brad summed up, "I think as far as our Christian living, what we practice on Sunday we try to do Monday through Saturday too. I think that's kind of important."

Lisa went on to tell me that since retiring, Brad has provided people with transportation to the doctor and to medical treatments. Usually, but not always, those he helps are church members. He pays the utility bill each month for a woman in the church on disability who has very limited resources, and he has also helped people with medical bills. She mused, "I feel strange telling this, because it's so private; I don't feel that's something you go around telling people." She explained that the Bible says there are various gifts, and they believe that sharing their financial resources is one of their gifts.

Brad noted that he had made pretty good money for somebody with just a high school education. He had to work hard, of course. Lisa had stayed home with the boys when they were small. But when they graduated from high school, she went to work, primarily so that she and Brad would have the means to support the church financially. That way, when tragedy strikes in others' lives, like a house fire, they have had the means to help. Brad said with a ring of pride in his voice, "I've noticed in the last few years that our boys help out friends if they're in trouble, or help them move or whatever they need." Before I met Brad and Lisa, I would have thought that a family who saw their spiritual gift to be that of providing financially for others would be those whom others would consider wealthy—bankers, businessmen, highly paid professionals. Here was a family where one spouse went to work specifically so that they would have the financial means to give money away.

Lisa went on to tell me that their oldest son, Jeff, noticed a teenage boy coming to work at his store with muddy shoes. Jeff learned that the boy was living in a lean-to in the woods outside of town. He had evidently been thrown out at home. So Jeff went into the woods and looked for the boy and took him home and prepared a room for him. The boy lived with Jeff and his wife for several weeks. Lisa mused, "I'm really very proud of them; I hope that Brad and I helped to instill some of that caring for others in them over the years." For all their quiet grumbling as teenagers, the boys have emulated their parents, developing eyes to see the needs of others and hearts called to giving and service.

Families and Faith

It did not take long for these stories to tumble out, scenes that this family thought would illustrate to a person from another planet what Christian faith is. Brad, Lisa, and Toby shared these stories of their living faith with me, a stranger, doing research on how faith informs the family life of Christians.[1] The research, which I dubbed the "Families and Faith Research Project," focused on learning what characterizes faith and spirituality in family life.

The Research

The project took place in four cities representing four diverse regions of the United States: the South, the Midwest, the Southwest, and the Pacific Northwest. I chose two congregations from each of four denominations (Southern Baptists, National Baptists, United Methodists, and Presbyterians USA) in each city.[2] The 32 congregations in the study are quite diverse; in size, they range from 98 congregants on an average Sunday to more than 1,200, with a median Sunday worship attendance of 225.

I interviewed 110 families in these congregations about their faith within the context of family life.[3] Either the pastor or a congregational committee helped select families for interview who represented both "peripheral" and "mainstay" members of the congregation. I also asked for families that represent the range of family types in their congregation (two parents with children, remarried families with children, single parents, single adults without children, childless couples, empty nest and senior adult singles and couples). Pastors alerted families I would be calling, asking for time to visit with them and their families to learn more about their faith-life together. As I scheduled visits with families I invited them to include "whoever your family is," whether or not they live in the same household.[4]

I spent two hours or so in the home of each family, listening to them tell me about their family life and their faith.[5] I had each interview recording transcribed, and I then studied those transcripts to understand how families experience and express their faith.[6] During the year following the interview, I sent a letter to each family thanking them and including in the letter a direct quotation from the interview and the meaning I believed that it had for understanding family life. I found this a helpful way to check the meaning I was deriving from the narratives they shared with me. Many of the families wrote back or called and thanked me for the opportunity to be interviewed; none suggested that the quotation in the letter had been misunderstood.

In addition, I held focus groups in two sites two years after the completion of the interviews. I invited several of the families in each site to participate in the focus groups. At the focus groups, I presented some of the themes that were emerging from the interviews and asked for their critiques.[7] Finally, I returned three years later for a second interview with twelve of the families, to see if what I had learned from them still held true.

Discoveries about Faith and Families

Our culture thinks of faith as a set of beliefs we hold as individuals, beliefs about God and Jesus and our relationship with God. Faith characterizes me; they are my beliefs. James Fowler has been the most influential researcher and theorist in exploring faith. His definition of faith emphasizes cognitive processes how persons understand their experiences and find meaning in them. He defines stages of faith that are congruent with human development theories, and that build on stage theories of cognitive and moral development. Fowler posits that there are universal stages of faith development, even though the content of faith varies greatly. In other words, all people have faith, because all people develop and revise frames of meaning, or ways of understanding their world.[8]

Several theorists have built on and challenged Fowler's theory of faith development. Craig Dykstra has suggested that faith should be defined not just cognitively, but as action that is grounded in a more or less conscious and chosen response to God's actions in the world. Faith is what persons *do*, not just what they believe.[9] It is Dykstra's description of faith as a way of life that framed my study of family faith. If faith is what we do in response to what we believe, then perhaps faith is expressed in what we do with our families, and not just how we act on our own.

The social sciences have taken a different approach in studying family systems and have found that families have shared beliefs, values, and practices, although these frameworks of meaning have not been called "family faith." For example, Hamilton McCubbin and his colleagues have studied the strength and resilience of families in many circumstances, including families who have lost members in wartime. McCubbin concluded that families have what he has called a "family schema," a set of beliefs, values, goals, priorities, and expectations they share for their relationship with one another and the larger community.[10] The question I began to ponder, then, is whether "family faith" could provide an alternative frame for studying family schema, at least in religious families. If so, does this schema, this family faith, in turn frame a family's action together as an expression of their shared faith? If so, then it would seem that we could identify family faith in the stories of their lives, of the actions they have taken with one another.

This looking for faith in the stories of family life counters our culture's understanding of faith as something we hold as individuals, however. We come into life as individuals, born into families. Even though we are surrounded by family, we also leave life as individuals—alone—through the doorway of death. Although we may accompany one another through life, we come and go alone. If faith is primarily what we believe, then foundationally, it is individual and not collective. Beliefs reside in our brains, and we do not have a collective brain, only individual ones. We may share a belief, but that sharing is based on what each of us individually believe that coincides with or is influenced by the beliefs of others.

What I learned from Brad, Lisa, and Toby, and from the other families that I interviewed is that faith is more than individual belief that carries us through life to death. Faith is the purpose that defines our life with one another, purpose that leads us to concerted action—to care for one another, and for neighbors and strangers. I listened for hundreds of hours as families told me about their experiences of

God in their lives together, and they told me, as did this family, not their set of beliefs, but their family stories. Beliefs are suppositions about what is true and what is not. Stories tell what truth is by showing how family members experience that truth in their daily lives. Nora Gallagher writes about wrestling with the crisis of a brother's death and of her call to ministry while she worked in a soup kitchen. In those experiences, she says that she came to understand faith not as believing, as the White Queen said to Alice in Wonderland, "six impossible things before breakfast."[11] Faith is the life we live that is full of more meaning than words can say, and that life is lived in the company of one another.

With the help of Brad and Lisa's family and the others I interviewed, as well as the experience of living in my own family, I came to understand faith as the melody of our lives. The songs we sing are far more than the written words and notes on a page. The melody, the music, gives the words life richer and deeper than printed statements can. We do not communicate faith just by spouting what we believe to be the central truths. We live it; it has to be illustrated. Like a song has to be sung to be music, so faith has to take shape in action, in doing. Family stories are like words sung to the melody of faith. One cannot fully explain what a story means except by telling it. One cannot describe a melody except by singing it.[12]

When I asked Brad and Lisa and Toby to teach me about the role of faith in their lives, they told me about wrestling furniture out of a rented truck into the home of a neighbor family on a snowy winter evening, of cutting lawns and wooden art objects to help out women who needed a financial boost, of taking sick neighbors to the doctor, of a son rescuing a homeless boy and providing him with a temporary home. They told me not so much about going to church together or the evening prayers they say together—although they do those things—but about caring for others beyond their family, together. The stories they told have so much more meaning than if they had tried to distill the stories into some central truth that shapes their lives, such as "do unto others as you would have them do unto you."

When Jesus was asked to teach, he told stories. Brad and Lisa could have quoted, chapter and verse, the teachings of Jesus that were core truths for them. But that was simply what they believed; their faith had to be told in stories of their life together. The melody of their lives is shared action, lived faith. The words of their stories include the seemingly mundane made sacred because they speak of service: wood saws, lawn mowers, used furniture, bits of cash for an unpaid bill, and making room for a stranger.

Brad's and Lisa's stories of service as the shared action that expresses their faith were not exceptions. In fact, *most* of the families I interviewed in the Families and Faith project talked about faith in the stories of their family life together, and many of those stories were about serving others in the community. Families talked about visiting patients dying of AIDS in a nursing home, about being the volunteer line-drawers on the community's soccer fields, about serving food in a free lunch program for homeless people, about taking in foster children. The list of ways these families were serving was long and as diverse as the families themselves. In their own ways, these Christians viewed serving together as families beyond their homes as the way they lived their faith.

In addition to service, families told me about faith in other melodies of their days together, the rituals and routines of life—meals together, bedtime prayers, sitting on a porch swing and watching summer sunsets. They included routine and special times of prayer together. They work in unity toward shared dreams and goals. Over and over, however, I found myself coming back to the remarkable sense of calling most families shared to get beyond their house walls in service to the larger community. There was something more compelling in their lives than just taking care of one another that held them together during the inevitable challenges and crises of life.

I hadn't expected families to define faith for me by telling me about their shared calling to serve. Our American understanding of Christian faith focuses on individual salvation, individual faithfulness, and individual vocation. These families led me into a broader understanding of what it means to be Christian. We are not just copilots with God on our life journey. We are traveling together in buses, as families and communities of families.

Biblical Narratives of Families and Faith

As important as a faith dimension of family life expressed in a shared calling to service seemed to be, I then began to ponder how what I had learned related to biblical perspectives on family life. I found myself reading the Bible with new eyes, looking for families that we might call "faithful" (there aren't many!) and how this phenomenon of service beyond themselves characterized their lives—or not. So many of the families of the Bible through whom God worked are deeply flawed, and so their stories sing the good news that God can use any family to accomplish God's purposes. The cast of characters includes Abraham, who attempted to make God's promises come true by starting a family with a slave at the request of his wife Sarah; it includes Leah and Rachel, two cowives and sisters in a fierce competition trying to bear the most baby boys for their shared husband; and it includes Tamar playing the part of a prostitute to maneuver her father-in-law into treating her with justice. And that is just a sampling![13] In the midst of these X-rated family shenanigans that are more about family flaws than family faith, three rather brief stories about families are quite different from the lifelong narratives of the more famous Bible families. These three families include Adam and Eve, Prisca and Aquila, and Ananias and Sapphira.

Adam and Eve's family story is infamous for their sin, their refusal to take responsibility (Gen 3:11-13), the consequent struggles that characterized their lives, and the pain of sibling rivalry leading to murder (Gen 4:1-8). The piece of their story that caught my attention, however, was *before* their fall into sin. What caught my attention was not what they did at all, but rather what God had intended their life together to be. I found it fascinating that the primary expectation from God had to do with what they would *do* together. The text actually does not mention the roles of lover and companion for one other. The first creation account just gives the simple command from God to "be fruitful," to populate and care for the good creation (Gen 1:28). In the second account of creation, God creates Eve because Adam needs a "helper" and none of the animals are suitable. Adam needs Eve to help him in the work of caring for the creation. Before the fall, then, family was called to work together, not just to be in a relationship with one another. The purpose of this first family was to care for all of God's good creation. We are one another's helpers in the work to which we are called.

Just as Adam and Eve are the creation family in the Old Testament, the first family we read about in the early church is the couple Prisca and Aquila. We hear nothing about their relationship with one another, or even if they were parents. What the writer focuses on and thus wants us to understand is their shared work, the way they lived their faith in service to others. They mentored and instructed others in the faith (Acts 18:26). They opened their home to others like Paul and hosted the church (Acts 18:3; 1 Cor 16:9). Paul writes that all the churches of the Gentiles gave thanks for them and their work, and he did especially, since Prisca and Aquila risked their necks for his life (Rom 16:4). We do not know exactly what they did for Paul or where they did it. We do know that Prisca and Aquila were working partners and are always listed together in the New Testament. No doubt they had individual gifts, but their names are so linked that they clearly had an important ministry partnership beyond what they did as individuals.

In stark contrast to Prisca and Aquila pouring out their lives for the community, Ananias and Sapphira, another couple we read about in Acts, conspired to appear as though they were giving of themselves when in fact they were holding out and contributing to their own hedge fund. With the full knowledge and support of his wife, Ananias sold a piece of land and gave a portion of the proceeds to the church, evidently proclaiming that he was giving it all when in fact he was secretly stashing away some of the proceeds. When confronted by Peter, he stuck to his lie. The seriousness of lying to the Holy Spirit resulted in Ananias collapsing and dying, as did his wife a few hours later when she told the same lie (Acts 5:1-11). This strange story seems to make the point that the purpose of family is to serve, not to put on the appearance of doing to cover our focus on family-centered nest feathering. Families who lose sight of a purpose more significant than their own lives together do so at their own peril.

If the melody of family life is faith lived in shared action, the words that go to that melody are the stories of service together—whether it is lugging household goods to a burned-out family or cutting the lawns or paying the medical bills of needy neighbors (Brad and Lisa's family); or whether it is caring for God's creation (Adam and Eve); or whether it is teaching as teams in the community of faith and folding others into our families for a time or for life (Prisca and Aquila—and Ms. Coper and her sons); or whether it is providing financially for the needs of the community of faith (Brad and Lisa, but not Ananias and Sapphira). Service appears to be central in the faith-life of Christian families. Perhaps Brad and Lisa and many of the other families I interviewed are unusual. After all, they were identified by their pastors for inclusion in a study of Christian faith and community service. Do the average folks in our congregations understand service as an important feature of their life together?

What "Average" Families in Our Congregations Tell Us

In addition to interviewing families in congregations, I have also been conducting surveys in congregations for twenty years. The survey instrument I have used, the "Church Census,"[14] is designed to help church leaders know more about the families they lead—the strengths of their families, the challenges and stresses they face, the ways they live their faith, and ways their church can help them.[15] Everyone in the church (from age twelve and up) is invited to take the survey, and it has provided us with rich information to guide congregational leaders. The survey has changed over time, as we listened to feedback from participating congregations. The last section of the survey was added in 2001 and is called simply, "How the church can help." The first version had forty-two topics in this section, such as communication skills; romance and sexuality in married life; romance and sexuality in single life; roles of men and women; managing time; managing money; family worship and prayer; coping with crises; parenting children; single parenting—and the list goes on. The survey asked respondents to "mark no more than three topics that you would like your church to help your family and other families with."

The list has grown gradually with each revision into the current version, which now has fifty-two items.[16] After the Families and Faith Research Project, we added one particular item to the Church Census section on how the church can help—"Help in serving others outside our family"—because of what we learned from Brad and Lisa and Toby and the other families in that study. In virtually every congregation we have surveyed since adding that item, we were amazed to discover that "Help in serving others" has been the most commonly named need by those who take the survey—more common than help with communication or marriage or conflict. We have surveyed Presbyterian, Lutheran, United Methodist, Southern Baptist, Cooperative Baptist, Unitarian, Episcopal, "Christian," Disciples of Christ, Church of God, and nondenominational congregations. Almost without exception, in the more than fifty congregations we have surveyed since adding that item, it is the most frequently named need in every congregation—help in serving others. These "average" families are asking their congregation's leaders to help them find ways to serve as families. All age groups—teenagers to senior adults—want the church to help their families serve.[17]

Of course, those are not the only concerns expressed. Teenagers asked for help with dating and romantic issues, communication skills, and with handling conflict and anger. Twenty-something adults asked for help managing money. Thirty- and forty-something adults asked for help parenting children and teenagers. Those in their fifties asked for guidance and help in caring for aging family members. But more often than all these other concerns was the surprising request to "help our family serve beyond ourselves." Every kind of family asked for help serving. Never-married adult families named it more often than items like dating, preparing for marriage, and romance and sexuality in single life. Divorced persons listed it more often than reconciliation and forgiving. Widowed families listed it more often than they did help with grief and coping with crises. Families living with major stress—financial, health, relational—still want to serve others.

It appears that even, and perhaps especially when our families are struggling, we need to know our lives together count for something.

What difference will it make that the Garland family lived in this community, this neighborhood? These church folks are saying that they want there to be more to their life together than keeping themselves economically solvent and physically healthy, loving one another and loving God, raising sturdy and happy children. Those goals are worthy and important, but they aren't enough.

In fact, we were surprised to find that a majority of the families surveyed with the Church Census are *already* engaged in service together in their communities. The survey includes a section entitled, "How we live our faith together." In one study we conducted of fifteen Baptist congregations, we found that families are more likely to be engaged in the world around them as expressions of their faith than to be engaged in studying the Bible together. The faith practices these Baptists reported that their families engaged in most often—besides going to worship services together—were serving others in need, caring for the created world, offering hospitality, seeking more justice in the world, and building stronger communities.[18]

Clearly families are already engaged in service together. Yet they are asking their congregations to guide them in that service. It is not as though it is hard to find a place to plug in and serve in our society. We are a society known for volunteering; opportunities are everywhere. Families can go to any number of social service agencies and find ample opportunities to serve their communities. There are a myriad of walks for various causes, community cleanups, and children's programs that need leaders. What these families said to us in the survey is that they want somehow to ground what they are doing in their lives of faith. They want their service to make sense as Christians.

Not just in spite of, but especially when life is hard, when health of a loved one is fragile, when our career dreams are shattered or a teenager goes off the rails, we need to know that our lives matter on a scale bigger than our home's floor plan. When exasperated spouses wonder if they made a mistake in marrying one another way back when, they need to know and remember that their lives are more than just their own. Families need to serve, to matter in the larger world, because God created them with a purpose.

Having a purpose beyond ourselves does not resolve the family crises. It does not fix the problems that might haunt us. But the purpose of our lives does give a frame for those crises and problems. It puts our family problems in perspective. Learning to handle conflict and anger in a Christian way, sharing thoughts and feelings deeply, encouraging and disciplining children to grow into the gifts God has placed in them—as important as these things are, they are not the central focus of the Christian life. Rather, they are ways families become equipped and resilient for the service to which they are called.

The Families and Faith Research Project ended, but I was left pondering the stories families told me about service in their communities, stories I hadn't really expected to hear. Then came the startling finding of the Church Census project that underscored the value families place on community service as an expression of their faith-life together. It was time to launch another project to learn more about how families are serving in their communities as their way of living their faith. How do families connect to the needs of their communities? How do they stay connected? What impact does their community involvement have on their family life and on their faith as individuals and as families? How are their congregations supporting them, or are they? How can congregations help families find their purpose together and make the connections between service and faith?

This time, a group of colleagues joined with me in the research.[19] We visited congregations across the United States and sat in the living rooms of families in those congregations that are involved in their communities.[20] What we learned changed how we think about church and how we think about being faithful as Christians. It even gave us new eyes for understanding the Christian story recorded in the New Testament and continuing to be lived today, in the lives of ordinary Christian families.

2

When Did We See You Hungry?

Then the righteous will answer him, "Lord, when did we see you hungry and feed you, or thirsty and give you something to drink? When did we see you a stranger and invited you in, or needing clothes and clothe you? When did we see you sick or in prison and go to visit you?"

The King will reply, "I tell you the truth, whatever you did for one of the least of these brothers of mine, you did for me." (Matt 25:37-40 NIV)

In chapter 1, we reported our surprise to learn that service beyond the house walls is central to the faith of the Christian families we have studied. That finding surprised us because when faith is discussed in our culture, it is often in terms of what we believe—a set of propositions we agree to, a creed we recite during worship together. If our definition of faith includes behaviors, those behaviors are often items such as frequency of church attendance, or personal prayer and Bible study. When this series of research studies of families and faith began, only one of the social scientific scales designed to study the way persons practice their faith included community service as a behavioral indicator of faith, or a "faith practice."[1]

When I was a child in the 1950s and 1960s, my Baptist church had its own version of a faith scale—the offering envelope. Each week, we carried our offering to church in an envelope that had a series of check-off boxes on the front. On that envelope, we recorded how we had lived our faith that week. Etched in my memory are the items: attended worship, showed up on time for Sunday school, brought an offering, brought my Bible, studied the Sunday school lesson. In essence, those envelopes were a personal faith practices scale. If I did those things, then I could consider myself "faithful."

Social sciences scales often have a short version—a few items that have been found statistically to represent the full scale. The essence of the full scale is distilled into a few items in the short version. The ultimate short version of the offering envelope faith practices scale was displayed proudly on one's chest—the attendance pin. That pin served as a quick indicator of the faith of the one wearing it. Those with perfect Sunday school attendance for a whole year received the pin. If you were truly sick, preferably contagious (chicken pox qualified), then the Sunday School Powers That Be might allow a perfect attendance pin even though you had one absence. If you made a whole second year of perfect attendance, then you got an extension to the pin. Each year of perfect attendance resulted in yet another extension to fasten, like rungs on Jacob's ladder, below the pin.

I remember that some of the older men in the church had a whole ribbon-length of pins hanging from the lapels of their church suits. Perhaps I am bitter about those pins, because I never received one. My parents always took us on a summer vacation trip in the family station wagon, often camping. If you attended church services at the campground or found a church where you were vacationing, then the attendance could count back in the home church toward the year's perfect attendance. As devout as my parents were, however, we did not often attend church on vacation. I never got a pin.

The envelopes and the pins were very effective ways to communicate what it means to be faithful. A half a century later, I can close my eyes and still picture one of those envelopes, when I have long forgotten so many other childhood experiences. Those envelopes still provide a snapshot of how our culture defines what it means to be faithful. The items focus on being a vital part of the Christian congregation—showing up, being prepared to participate in its programs, supporting it financially. What was not included in the envelope scale was life outside the congregation. Service outside the church walls has been considered elective in American church life, not essential.[2]

The disconnection of faith practices—summarized by congregations' offering envelopes—with Christian religious thought about the centrality of service in the Christian life is striking. Many leading voices in Christian thought in the United States see faith and community ministry as inextricably linked.[3] According to the Protestant reformer Martin Luther, faith and service are so closely related that they are as impossible to separate as are a fire's heat and its light.[4] Service is not elective for Christian life, something we add on to a core of worship attendance and financial giving and Bible study. Service is at the very heart of what it means to walk the Christian way. When Peter vowed his love for Jesus, Jesus responded, "feed my lambs" (John 21:15-17). If we love the Good Shepherd, we live that love by caring for the sheep.

Our surveys tell us how important service is to Christian families, even though most congregations still have not replaced the offering envelope faith practices scale with a version that includes service. If we connect service to the faith practices of congregations, it will take more than our family surveys, however. We need to speak to Christians and their congregations in the language of faith. The language of Christian beliefs and values are embedded in biblical teaching, not what we can learn with the tools of the social sciences. Our research suggests that engaging families in service will strengthen their faith, will strengthen their life commitments to one another, will do all matter of good for them. But as church leaders, we lead Christians into caring for the sheep because that is what it means to be Christian. To connect service with faith as it is depicted in congregation life, we have to connect what we have learned about the role of service in the family life of Christians with the biblical themes and narratives of Christian faith.

Stories are particularly powerful in shaping our understanding of God, our world, and ourselves. The meaning of Bible stories is seldom transparent or unidimensional, and so they provide rich opportunity for community conversation, conflict, and deeper understanding over time. These stories invite us to wonder and explore, and then to struggle with how the stories connect with our own life stories. Stories communicate truths that cannot be captured by a proverb. For example, "If you close your ear to the cry of the poor, you will cry out and not be heard" (Prov 21:13), speaks truth. It does not hit us with the same power, however, as the story Jesus told of the end of times, when the Son of Man will separate sheep from goats based on how they responded to persons who are hungry or thirsty or estranged or imprisoned, persons who are actually the unrecognized presence of God in the midst of our lives (Matt 25). The story haunts us, stays with us more than the proverb, even though they both speak the same truth: that God expects us to care for those in need around us, and we risk our own peril if we ignore that expectation.

The First Church

The stories of the leaders of the early church, like the stories of the families I interviewed, say so much more than the words "Service is the heart of Christian faith." These stories provide rich fodder for chewing on together as we consider the role of service in a life of faith.

One such story that has challenged my thinking about faith and service is the way the early church handled its own ministry with the community. The role of community service in the life of synagogues was already in place when the first church came into being. Synagogues in Jesus' day often organized their charity into a first-century version of the soup kitchen and collected a charity fund for needy members.[5] The early church carried on the synagogue tradition of feeding the hungry. As the church grew rapidly and began crossing cultural divides, however, so the kitchen ministry grew and groaned with strife. Greek-speaking members of that early church complained of discrimination, that their widows were getting shorted in the food distribution. The twelve disciples—the church leaders—considered the ensuing conflict to be an unwelcome distraction from more important church business. They said to each other, "It is not right that we should neglect the word of God in order to wait on tables" (Acts 6:2a). They decided to delegate the responsibility, and so Stephen and Philip and six other men were chosen to serve in the feeding ministry. These men were to handle this bothersome ministry to the community of poor widows, preferably, it would seem, at some distance from where the church leaders were studying the word of God and praying (Acts 6:4).

This development in the early church is particularly interesting when juxtaposed with an experience these same disciples had with Jesus just a short time before Jesus' death and resurrection. The Gospel of Mark reports that toward the end of Jesus' ministry, they were walking through Galilee and Jesus was explaining to the disciples that he was about to be betrayed and killed, but that he would rise again (Mark 9:30-31). The disciples, not understanding, were afraid to ask him to explain further (v. 32). Instead, they turned the focus of their attention to themselves. Perhaps they were trying to understand what the ending of Jesus' ministry would mean for them. "If that's where this is going to end, then what will happen to us?" That is what I would have been thinking, had I been in their place. From there, the conversation must have turned to what their respective positions would be in the culmination of Jesus' ministry. That conversation must have degenerated into an argument about which of them was the most important (v. 34). When they reached their destination that evening, Jesus asked them what they had been discussing out on the road and these normally talkative men became strangely silent. I can imagine that in their embarrassment they averted their eyes; some of them looked at their feet, others were suddenly quite distracted and focused on something in the distance—anything but Jesus' question. Jesus knew full well that they had been arguing, and what they had been arguing about, and uttered his memorable line in response: "Whoever wants to be first must be last of all and servant of all" (v. 35). To make his point about what it really means to be first, to be the "greatest" as the disciples had been discussing, he took a child into his arms and said: "Whoever welcomes one such child in my name welcomes me, and whoever welcomes me welcomes not me but the one who sent me" (v. 37).

Just prior to their argument, Jesus had been explaining the kingdom of God to them, a kingdom founded on his willingness to give his own life and to be humiliated and killed, with the promise of being raised again in ultimate victory. But when they did not understand Jesus' version of the "end of the story," they created their own version of the ending, jockeying for and arguing over their respective places of prestige—of greatness—in the kingdom to come that Jesus had been describing. It would be interesting to know what criteria the disciples were using to argue about their own greatness. Was it who was the most articulate speaker, the most effective healer, or who could raise the most money for the cause? We do not know, but it clearly was not the same definition of greatness that Jesus had in mind. It was not serving the least important members of society. It was in this context of trying to teach his followers about how to order their relationships with one another that Jesus brought a little person, a nobody in the contest for greatness, into the very center, saying, "If you want to be great, if you want to welcome God into your lives, then be servants; seek out and care for the nobodies, the littlest and least important."

The disciples still did not understand—or did not *want* to understand—what Jesus was trying to teach them. In the very next chapter of Mark (10:13-14), people were bringing their children to Jesus for his blessing, and the disciples tried to shove them aside. They said, in essence, "We've got important business to be about; don't bother us with children." Don't bother us with those who have nothing to offer us, who aren't somebodies with power or resources we can use. This time Jesus was aggravated with them, or the Bible says, he was "indignant." He told them yet again to let the little people come straight on to him, to stop getting in their way. In fact, there is not only room enough and time enough for the little ones, but indeed, Jesus explained that they are the very heart of God's concern. The kingdom belongs to them.

Fast forward to the early church in Acts 6. These same disciples had now reached the positions of spiritual prominence they had imagined on that walk with Jesus. They were the church's leaders, carrying on the work of Jesus, now dead and raised again and gone on before them. They were the same ones who had argued on that road, walking behind Jesus, about who was the greatest—the ones who later tried to push parents with children aside as unimportant. Now they were trying to organize this church bursting at the seams with new growth. For all that they had been through since that walk with Jesus, they still seemed to be having the same conversation with the same outcome that had made Jesus indignant.

The work of feeding the community, little people, small in the eyes of the world because they were poor, was troubling the disciples. People were squabbling. So, the apostles came up with a brilliant idea. Let's get a few good men—other than us—to run the social ministry, men who understand these different ethnic groups in our midst. They believed that they could not allow their leadership to be distracted with these unimportant people—widows and poor folks. They needed to be able to devote themselves to prayer and to "serving the word" (Acts 6:4). They still did not understand Jesus' lesson—that the little ones, the poor, the children and widows, are not a distraction. They are the main focus of Jesus' attention, and so they should be the main focus of his followers.

Stephen was one of those men the church chose to do the food ministry. And while the apostles were doing whatever their ministry of prayer and the word involved, Stephen not only served tables, but also delivered the longest sermon in the book of Acts (chapter 7) and became the first among them—first to follow Jesus into death. Stephen lived the greatness Jesus had told them about. The Holy Spirit sent Philip, one of the others set aside for community ministry, to share the gospel with and baptize the Ethiopian eunuch, and to carry the news about the Messiah to the Samaritans (Acts 8:4-5). It appears that while the church leaders were closeted at home, trying to focus on praying and studying God, Stephen and Philip were demonstrating the lesson that Christianity is about service, especially to those who are poor, strangers, or culturally different.

The disciples tried to separate ministry to the little ones, the nobodies, from the spiritual disciplines of prayer and study about God. They continued to miss Jesus' teaching that prayer and knowledge of God and serving the little people of this world are a seamless whole. Knowing God and caring for neighbors is not a task to be delegated. It was Stephen and Phillip who focused on embracing the world outside the church community. It was Stephen who stood and preached, and while he did, everyone saw how his face was like that of an angel (Acts 6:15). The picture of Stephen's glowing face calls to memory the other man in the Bible whose face glowed—Moses. Moses' face glowed after talking with God, and the people were afraid to come near him (Exod 34:29-30). Moses' face glowed because he had seen God, and now Stephen's face was aglow. From Jesus' teaching, we realize that Stephen had been with God's presence because he had been with the "little ones," with the needy, and whoever welcomes a little one welcomes God. While Philip and Stephen went about their ministry to the marginalized, they were *experiencing God*—hearing and seeing God firsthand. Stephen saw God in the moments before he was martyred (Acts 7:56). Philip heard God's voice through an angel, directing him to teach the Ethiopian (Acts 8:26).

It is easy to call the disciples dense, to marvel at their inability to grasp the seemingly straightforward teaching of Jesus that we experience God by serving others, especially people the world considers powerless or unimportant. I am not at all convinced, however, that we have grasped Jesus' teaching any better than the disciples did. Jesus was saying to put children—representing the powerless and marginalized in any age—first in the life of our faith community. If the church wants to be "great," then our biggest concern ought to be making service to the smallest in our society the central organizing function of our life together.

Jesus was talking to the future leaders of his church about making *experiencing God* the central focus of their life together. He said, in essence, that it is with the children, the "little people" of this world, that we can find God. If you want to know God, to see Jesus, bring one of God's needy children to the center of what you do. In other words, Christians' motivation for caring for the shut-out, unimportant people of this world is not simply that they need our care. Quite the contrary, we need them.

We miss the point if we think our service is, foundationally, a way to meet needs that will otherwise go unmet. Psalm 147 teaches that the God who can cause the stones to speak and who throws the stars in space and names each one can take care of little people in our world. God will bind up their wounds. It is our privilege to be able to join God in caring, because in doing so, we find God. God can—and will—roll down justice like a river without us (Amos 5:24). Stephen was just running a feeding ministry for poor people in the community. There he encountered God; there he found his voice, empowered by God, and he was the first to follow the steps of Jesus. When he did, he saw Jesus *stand up* to call him into the kingdom. Two of the disciples' mother, before his arrest, had asked Jesus to let her sons sit next to him in his coming kingdom (Matt 20:20-22); they wanted to be the greatest. They were concerned about their position in the kingdom. "Can we sit in positions of power next to you, Lord?" But Stephen did not have to ask where his place would be. In the last moments of his life, he *saw* his place. It was not a place to sit—it was a Lord standing up to welcome him home. "Look," he said, "I see heaven open and the Son of Man standing at the right hand of God" (Acts 7:56).[6]

The Prophet Micah

The connection between faith and service in the Christian life builds on the ancient Hebrew prophet Micah's understanding of God's expectations. Micah's prophecy is deceptively simple, with not a word about what we should believe:

> With what shall I come before the Lord, and bow down before God on high? Shall I come before him with burnt offerings, with calves a year old? Will the Lord be pleased with thousands of rams, with ten thousand rivers of oil? Shall I offer my firstborn for my transgression, the fruit of my body for the sin of my soul? He has told you, O mortal, what is good; and what does the Lord require of you but to do justice, and to love kindness and to walk humbly with your God? (Micah 6:6-8)

To Do Justice

Micah is clear: God is not pleased by people organizing elaborate worship practices. For Micah, those worship practices involved sacrifices of living things and of precious oil poured out in worship. God does not want our guilt-ridden attempts to make up for the wrongs we have done. Instead, God wants us to seek justice. Justice means equal opportunities for all God's people. Justice refers to the teaching, found in Leviticus (25:10-28), to practice the economic system of Jubilee spelled out in Yahweh's instruction to Moses.

Those instructions were explicit about how to manage wealth and poverty, how to care for the earth and for neighbors, all wrapped into the concepts of Sabbath and Jubilee. Every seventh *day* was to be a Sabbath, a day of rest. Every seventh *year* was to be a Sabbath year. Then, not only are people supposed to rest, but the land was supposed to be allowed to rest, too. Yahweh promised that there would be a bumper crop in the sixth year so that there would be plenty to eat for two years, allowing the land and the people a yearlong rest. Moreover, every seventh Sabbath year—seven times the seven years, or forty-nine years—the people were to proclaim it the Year of Jubilee. In that year, not only were the land and the people to rest, but they were to redistribute the money and the land. The people of Yahweh lived in a rural economy; they depended on crops. Sometimes farmers fell into debt and had to sell their land in order to pay their bills, leaving them no way of supporting themselves. Sometimes poor people even had to sell themselves as slaves because they could not pay their bills. But in the Year of Jubilee, every forty-nine years, people who had sold their land were supposed to have it returned to them. People who had sold themselves into slavery out of economic desperation were to be set free.

By the time of Jesus, there is no evidence that Jubilee had ever really been operationalized, people being people. The rich simply got richer, and the poor poorer. Then came Jesus, and the first sermon out of his mouth proclaimed "the year of the Lord's favor"—Jubilee (Luke 4:16-21). The good news Jesus brought was that the time had come, the time to set free the poor, to put things right, to do away with the poverty that had grown in the land, the inequality. That was—and is—the good news.

Sometimes we get confused and think that America's democratic economic system is Christian. But God's economic institution is Jubilee, a way of protecting and caring for the smallest and weakest in society. God says, "You cannot sell land or accumulate wealth permanently, because it belongs to me; you are simply my guests; I want to be sure everyone gets a fair chance." In a rural economy, every family needed land in order to have a chance. Jubilee meant that the economic troubles of one generation of families would not condemn their children to poverty. Every fifty years, a new generation got a fresh start, an even start.

Our society values acquiring as much as a person can and holding on to it. Parents are responsible for their own children's futures, and if they are poor and cannot provide, then children suffer. In fact, our society is living the reverse of Jubilee. We are an Eelibuj society.[7] "Eelibuj" is Jubilee turned backward. Today, the wealthiest one percent of Americans have more money and property than the bottom 95 percent combined. The poorest families are families with children—families who are struggling to provide a future for the next generation. This is true in our society, and it is true all over the world, and it is becoming even more so. The richer are getting richer, and the poor are becoming destitute. As one woman in a congregation where I was speaking on children and poverty said to me in all candor, "I didn't breed 'em, and I shouldn't have to feed 'em." Poor little ones are not our responsibility, according to our culture.

In the late summer of 2005, Hurricane Katrina exposed the stark realities of poverty in the United States. In that massive natural disaster that destroyed much of New Orleans and the Gulf Coast, we saw who suffered the most, who was left behind, who waited in vain for help to arrive, until some died there. Those left behind were overwhelmingly poor and people of color, the very old and the very young—the little ones. They were the ones who could not leave; who had no cars or money for gas; who had no money for the bus; who had no friends or family with room in their cars to spare. They were already poor before the storm; now they were totally exposed and on their own. For days, nobody came for them.

Our nation was shocked. Most folks did not realize how many Americans were poor. The waters washed away the veneer to reveal the underside of America. We saw poor mothers with their babies stranded on rooftops crying for help, or jammed into a dangerous and dirty sports arena waiting for days for water and food. We heard of frail elderly persons left to drown. Too little help came too late for too many little ones. In its reporting on the hurricane, the mainstream media focused on poverty in the United States in a way it had not in years, in blanket coverage that lasted days. We heard that New Orleans had a child poverty rate of almost 50 percent. That rate was only a little higher than other major cities and actually a little lower than some others. It did not take long, however, for the news to turn to other events in the world. And people being people, we let that horror slip from the forefront of our thoughts and conversations.

The words of Micah call us to do justice, to minister not only to the needs of persons who have been hurt by society's injustice, but to speak out against unjust systems themselves. Those systems include an economy that allows God's children to live in poverty and homelessness, a commercial system that perverts our values through an omnipresent media, a government system that allows the loudest voices to control the national budget at the expense of voiceless children, poor people, and immigrant strangers, and a system of societal values that promotes "me first" and leaves children and poor people and strangers last.

To Love Kindness

Second, God calls us to "love kindness"—in some translations the word is "mercy"—meaning to extend care to those in need. In addition to working for justice, we are to care for the one in front of us who is in need right now, who cannot wait for a more just society. The need is now. Justice says that everyone needs to be able to earn a livable wage that provides the resources for sufficient food and clothing and shelter. While we are working toward a just society with livable wages, though, mercy gives a spare shirt to someone who does not have one.

In the novel told around a true event, *Blue Hole Back Home*, Joy Jordan-Lake tells the story of a group of teenagers growing up in a Southern mountain town who befriend the "new girl," a teenager from Sri Lanka whose family moved there with the hope that America might be a land of promise for them. As a member of the only dark-skinned family in town, the young girl is shunned by the "cool" teenagers in the community. But a motley group of not-cool kids invites her to the community's swimming hole. As a consequence, not only are they shunned along with her, but insidious messages of racism begin to gather like clouds. Names are called; fires are set. Doggedly, the group tightens their care for one another all the way through a tragic and yet victorious end. All of us have been teenagers wanting desperately to be "cool," to be considered "in." Being the friend to someone when the association can paint you as "not cool" is what it means to love kindness. The "new girl" could not wait for an end to racism in this country; she was a teenager right then, in need of friends who would make a place for her in an unkind society. The word "kindness" is related to "kin." To love kindness is to treat others as kin-folk, family. You are my brother, my sister. What I have is yours.

To Walk Humbly with Your God

The third call of Micah is to walk humbly with our God. Our work for justice and our acts of kindness are done in humility, always in the context of our relationship with God. Professor Page Kelly, a colleague of mine in Kentucky long ago, taught me that walking humbly with God means keeping in step with God. Keeping in step implies taking a walk, being on a journey. We are walking in step with a God that has always not only cared for the little people but has also used little people—like us—to accomplish mighty deeds. He used two Jewish midwives to save a generation of babies, including Moses, who would lead the people out of Egypt (Exod 1:15-21). Those two women in a traditionally female occupation had the strength to defy Pharaoh not because they were strong women, but because they were keeping in step with God. God does not call us to be awesome. God calls us to be willing to give what we have so that God can work through us, speak through us, and change the world through us.

The "ought" of Christian faith is not difficult to state; but it is difficult to live. It requires making service the heart of our faith. Working for justice and caring for the needs of others are not optional choices in a buffet of spiritual practices from which we can pick and choose. They are not distractions from a more "spiritual way." They are *the* way. We are walking the road with Jesus, after all, and he told us what was expected if we really are serious about being his followers, about being good news.

Schindler's List

It is not only the stories of the Bible but also the stories of people's lives that can help us grasp the depth of the truth that, for Christians, true greatness comes through serving the "least of these." The movie *Schindler's List* became a cultural event that had profound meaning to persons a generation or more removed from the atrocities of the Holocaust. The film told the true story of German businessman Oskar Schindler who, during World War II, went to Nazi-occupied Poland looking for economic prosperity. A charming, sly entrepreneur bent on personal gain, he befriended and bribed the Nazi authorities to gain control of a factory in Krakow. He staffed his factory with Jewish slave laborers and soon was making a fortune.

His plant manager, Itzhak Stern, was also a Jewish slave. Stern saw to it that Schindler's workforce included the most vulnerable members of Krakow's Jewish community, who without work would be sent to their death in the concentration camps. In spite of himself, as he worked day by day with Stern and the Jewish workforce Stern had recruited, Schindler grew to feel empathy and then responsibility toward his workers. When the Nazis confined all the Jews remaining in the ghetto to a forced labor camp, Schindler volunteered to keep "his Jews" confined at the factory. At his own expense, this man who set out to be a war profiteer was constructing barracks and stringing barbed wire, appearing to create an outpost of the labor camp that in reality was a safe haven. In the end, Schindler spent everything he had to "buy" as many Jews as possible, becoming the savior of more than 1,100 Jews. Oskar Schindler was transformed by caring for his neighbors, who came to call themselves the *Schindlerjüden* ("Schindler's Jews").

Schindler's List was a powerful movie, only in part because of its connection with the historical event of the Holocaust. Its power goes beyond the historical event, however, because all of us can identify with Oskar Schindler. If that ordinary, self-centered, self-indulging, care-less human was transformed in the act of giving himself for others, coming even to risk his own life, then there is hope for us, too. Schindler transcended his self-centeredness not by thinking his way out of it or believing his way out of it or willing his way out of it, but rather simply by being drawn into service to others.

Christianity is a *Schindler's List* kind of faith. It is not just a set of beliefs about God, the world, and ourselves that if we get right, then we are "in." Robert Coles has said that the essence of spirituality is the human capacity to wonder about things and to try to figure them out; spirituality includes the intellectual activity of moral reasoning. Even if I am able to think morally about life's important questions, that is simply a critique about my intellectual life; it does not mean I am living faithfully.[8]

If it is not about the intellectual life, then neither is Christianity simply a life controlled by a set of rules and constraints—tell the truth; go to church regularly; be nice to other people. It is not a life of prayer and study at the center, with service as an outflowing of an inner life centered in relationship with God. Instead, discipline and study and prayer and service are woven indistinguishably into a whole cloth. Our beliefs should lead us into service; otherwise they are useless and lifeless—dead (Jas 2:14-26). It is as we serve, putting our faith to work, that our faith deepens and strengthens. Prayer and study should lead us to service, and service sends us to our Bibles for comfort and challenge and the connection of our story to *the* story. Service sends us to our knees in prayer for others, for ourselves, for the broken places in our world.

If faith and service are so integrally connected to one another, as exhorted by Scripture and exemplified by the stories of the early church and in the lives of heroes like Oskar Schindler, are regular Christians making this connection today? The families in this research project helped me to see that the relationship between service and faith is actual lived reality in the lives of "ordinary" Christians in today's world.

Ordinary American Christians

Our research team studied thirty-five congregations scattered across the country, chosen because they were known for being involved in service to their communities. We surveyed whole congregations and interviewed leaders and members engaged in community service to see what we could learn about the connection these Christians made between their lives of faith and their involvement in community service.[9] Altogether, we surveyed 7,300 respondents in the thirty-five congregations. Of those, 850 respondents reported that they were currently involved in volunteer (unpaid) community service.

The surveys showed that those involved in service to their community reported that they prayed, attended worship services, and gave significantly more (financially) than those not involved in service. In fact, being involved in community service as often as once a week or more was significantly related to other measures of faith, such as prayer and Bible study. Active engagement in service to others had a more profound relationship with the faith of these ordinary Christians than any other faith activity, including attending congregational worship. This finding was true for adults, and it was also true for the 631 teenagers we surveyed. Community service was significantly more closely related to the faith development of teens than attending worship services. In short, we found that *service is the most significant and powerful contributor* to faith for teenage and adult Christians.

For the Sake of Our Children

Other researchers have also discovered that service is strongly related to teenagers' faith. In fact, service appears to be more powerful than Sunday school, Bible study, or participation in worship in the faith development of teenagers. Young people who are involved in service that is connected to their faith are much more likely to be firmly bonded to their churches and are much less likely to drop out of school.[10] In a survey of Catholic youth, 63 percent reported it was opportunities for service that had attracted them to participate in their parish's youth program.[11] Our children want to serve, and in turn, service strengthens their faith.

If service is so important to Christian faith, it is remarkable that it is not as central to the lives of congregations as worship and Bible study. Sadly, a Gallup survey of adolescents found that only 20 percent said they were involved in activities sponsored by their congregation "to help less fortunate people," and an additional 60 percent said they would *like* to be involved in such service. Based on data from the 2002–2003 National Study of Youth and Religion, Smith and Denton noted that only 30 percent of adolescents have ever been involved by their congregation in a mission team or service project. That is compared to 50 percent of U.S. teenagers who have been to a youth retreat or conference.[12] How much staff time and budget dollars in our congregations are spent on Bible study and worship? And how much on involving children and adults in service as an expression of faith? The vast majority of congregations devotes very small percentages of their energies to serving in their communities, and then in relatively minor projects peripheral to the congregation's life together. When they do serve, congregations mainly help to meet emergency needs in a way that involves minimal contact between the congregational volunteers and those in need. Only 6 percent of congregations have a staff person devoting at least 25 percent of his or her time to leading the congregation's social service.[13]

The Kind of Service Matters

We also learned that the relationship of faith and service is affected by the nature of the service that Christian youths and adults engage in. The surveys taught us that a growing faith is particularly associated with involvement in service with persons who are different—from different cultures and life experiences—bringing to mind the Greek widows in the early church community. We are stretched to new understandings of ourselves and of God when we have to work at understanding someone whose life experiences are different from our own, and who perhaps has a different perspective on the world and its Creator.

We also learned that faith can grow in one-shot service opportunities—building a house for a poor family, serving food in a homeless feeding program, handing out food vouchers or groceries. But

Christian faith is strengthened much more in service opportunities that allow people to develop relationships with one another. A one-week mission trip can be a powerful educational experience, but the real faith development comes in sharing a portion of our time week by week, over time—delivering meals to frail elderly adults every week, learning their birthdays and celebrating with them, and finding that we are receiving just as much or more as we are giving. Those serving are essentially bringing these "little ones" of our culture to the center of their concern, and as a consequence, they find their own lives changed.

Service often pushes volunteers into situations and expectations that are beyond the familiar, and sometimes it can be overwhelming. It can drive volunteers to prayer in search of ways to deal with situations they have never encountered before. One church leader we interviewed explained that service recipients can be frustrating and have the potential to make would-be helpers feel helpless: "Their problems are too complex; their families are too broken; their thinking seems too distorted—you can't fix this on your own." In the face of not knowing what to do or how to help, we learn that sometimes problems cannot be fixed simply—or at all. Volunteers learn tenacious caring for people regardless of their life choices and, in the process, to rely more fully on God. We are compelled to pray when we do not know what else to do. A volunteer who works with homeless families said, "If I actually know people who are not going to make it, are not going to stay out of jail, or are not going to get off drugs unless God does a miracle, then I pray, because that's all we've got."

The people we interviewed had been engaged in volunteer community service for at least a year, and many for far longer. They told us that as they served, their understanding about the nature of "success" had changed. Christine, now in her 80s, had been working for more than ten years in a homeless shelter for women, where she taught the women how to make and keep to a budget. She still remembers the first woman she counseled, because the experience transformed her own life. The woman did not make it out of her overwhelming circumstances; she ended up back on drugs and on the street. Christine said, "She had a huge impact on me, and I thought right then and there that I have to rethink what success means. Success doesn't mean persons' problems are solved or they absolutely make it back into a healthy, independent lifestyle. For me it just simply means that I show up every week and give them my full attention for that time." She puts the people she serves at the center of her concern.

Christine learned to redefine success as her own faithfulness to "show up," as she said. Volunteers often said that they feel inadequate to the task, but that they have learned to do what they can and trust God for the outcome. In short, they redefined the desired outcome of their service. Success did not necessarily mean life changes in those they served. Rather, they saw that success was really about themselves, about their own behavior of being consistently present—being faithful. In the process of serving, then, they found themselves changed. As they were faithful to be present even when they could not improve the lives of those they served, they learned to care for them. A woman teaching English as a Second Language classes for Mexican immigrants described how easy it is to judge others if we do not know what their lives have been like. She went on to say, "I am learning to see people as God sees them, to have understanding and compassion."

These servant Christians sometimes hesitated and struggled when we asked them to describe the results of volunteering in their own lives. They had to think about it, because self-change was not their motivation for serving. They had started out wanting to give, not really thinking about receiving; to help others make life changes, not to be changed themselves. They were surprised by the mutual benefits of their serving. The benefits to the volunteers, including a change in their own faith-life, are *results*, not motives for serving, and it is important not to confuse the two. Christians do not seek the opportunity to serve others because it will deepen their faith. They serve simply because that is what it means to be a Christian.

A new wind is blowing. Congregational leaders are recognizing that if they want congregations to grow, they have to turn their congregations inside out and involve their people in service to their communities. They are realizing they need to focus on living their faiths more than increasing worship attendance. Leaders of what has come to be known as "the externally focused church movement" suggest that the effectiveness of congregational leadership should not be measured by what happens inside the church "but rather by the impact the people of the church have on their communities."[14] They suggest that the most significant factor in growing a strong, resilient faith is being involved from the very beginning in service to others in the community. Too many American Christians keep looking for a spiritual "fix," going from one Bible study group to another to retreats to the latest Christian book, hoping to find what will give them meaning and purpose, without realizing that it is in giving self in service that they will find the fulfillment they seek. We were created "for good works" and it is in that doing good that we find our place as God's handiwork (Eph 2:10):

> The purpose of the church should be more than "body" building. The church should be more like a training facility designed to equip the saints for works of service. . . . The church is a place of rehabilitation, not convalescence. It is not a hospice that prepares people to die; it is a rehab center preparing people to live.[15]

Serving as a Family Affair

Our research project focused initially on Christians serving as individuals. What we did not expect to find was that many of these Christians did not see service as something for them to do alone; they were serving alongside family members. Couples prepared food together to feed persons who are homeless; they served together in meals-on-wheels and took their grandchildren with them; parents involved their own children in evening recreational programs for inner-city children where they served as leaders. Even though their congregations envisioned these service opportunities for individuals, these servant Christians were quietly making it a family service activity.[16]

A Search Institute study of Protestant congregations found that involvement in *family* service projects during childhood and adolescence has a powerful impact on young people's growth in faith. In fact, about one-third of Protestant youth are actually involved in service with their families.[17] It seems that families are more likely to involve their young people in service than their congregations, and that is encouraging, because parents are the single most important influence on the spiritual lives of adolescents.[18] Even if teenagers and their parents are not very aware of this fact, parents are vitally important. They are more important even than the congregation's youth group in the shaping of faith. The research is clear; if you want to know what the religious and spiritual lives of adolescents will look like in the future, then look at the religious and spiritual lives of their parents today.[19]

From his research on the roots of kindness and caring, Robert Wuthnow concludes that caring is not an innate characteristic established at birth. We learn it, and we learn it first in family life. Parents model for their children, both in their family relationships and in relationships with others in the community, the kindness that youths then emulate in the world around them. In fact, Wuthnow has suggested the small acts of kindness of daily family life are probably most significant, showing as they do that caring is not terribly difficult or exceptional but can be a "natural" part of life.[20] It is a life together that carries over into relationships beyond the house walls—taking a church member to the doctor, cutting a neighbor's lawn, quietly helping a disabled widow with a utility bill. Families interviewed in the Families and Faith study, like Lisa and Brad, often did not talk much about what they were doing as an outpouring of their faith. As one senior adult said about faith, "We don't talk about our faith—we just do it."

This connection between service and faith takes on added meaning because of the kind of world we live in, a world that is very focused on the realm of work. We define ourselves by the occupations we hold. American Christians tell our teenagers they are loved, but they may not feel particularly needed in a society that has emphasized children's dependence on adults for care and support. The U.S. tax code says it clearly—they are "dependents." The standard question we ask children when attempting to form a relationship with them is what they want to be when they grow up, implying that they have to grow up to be somebody, to have an identity. We define people by the jobs they have—or will have someday. Only two generations ago, children had a vital role to play in family life—working on the farm alongside adults, caring for younger siblings, contributing to the overall life of the family. In today's world, most of the "real" work takes place away from home. If teenagers have part-time jobs, it is most likely to make their own spending money or perhaps to help with school expenses, but not to contribute to the overall well-being of the family or community.

There is no deeper poverty than having nothing to give to others, and in that sense, our kids are growing up impoverished, even and probably especially our middle-class kids. Jack Calhoun has pointed out that involving kids in service alongside adults broadens the definition of good from *being* good to something more muscular, namely, to *doing* good.[21] Being involved in serving others and working for justice gives meaning to life right now. Children can be good news in the lives of others right now; their calling to Christian service is not on hold until they reach adulthood.

In the Families and Faith study, I stumbled onto families like Brad and Lisa's who had centered their lives together in quiet service to their community as the way they lived their faith and passed on their faith to their children. Clearly, service has a profound impact not only on the lives of Christians, but also on family life.

3

The Path into Family Ministry
Chutes and Ladders

Heather and Jim Hall have been married almost twenty years. They belong to a nondenominational congregation of more than three thousand members. Jim is a chemical engineer, head of a large division of a petroleum company. Heather is a physical therapist in the Catholic hospital. Their three children, Marianne (15), Jonas (11), and Sarah (8), all attend the private Christian school sponsored by their church.[1]

The Halls have been very active in their congregation. Heather teaches Sunday School and Jim serves as an elder. Both of them have taken off from work to lead in the congregation's summer Vacation Bible School. A year ago, though, Heather became restless and worried that they were not doing enough to nurture faith in their children. She wanted more in their lives as a Christian family than going to church in the same car. They had read Bible stories to their children when they were preschoolers, but now that they were all in school the bedtime story routine was long past. The brief prayer at the supper table was really the only evidence, other than going together to church activities, identifying their family life as "Christian."

First Heather tried reading a passage of Scripture together before or after supper—when they had a chance to eat together in the pressure of all the soccer practices and music lessons and church and school activities. But no one had much patience for Bible reading when they were hungry and the food was getting cold right before their eyes. After supper did not work any better; the children wanted to get on with playing outdoors or doing homework or talking to friends on the phone. They sat obediently, but Marianne silently rolled her eyes and Jonas and Sarah fidgeted. It felt forced, and so, discouraged, Heather abandoned her attempt at "family prayer time."

One Sunday, the Scripture read during the church worship service was 1 Peter 4:8-10:

> Above all, maintain constant love for one another, for love covers a multitude of sins. Be hospitable to one another without complaining. Like good stewards of the manifold grace of God, serve one another with whatever gift each of you has received.

The passage hit Heather with such power that she remembers it more than a year later. The theme of the sermon that morning was that serving is not simply one of several possible spiritual gifts. Rather, serving is required of every Christian, even though our differing gifts may suggest different ways that we can love our neighbors as ourselves. Heather listened intently. She prayed for God to use her gifts, and as she did, she was struck that the most important gift in her life was her family of healthy, energetic children and her loving partner in parenting and in life. How might God want her to use her gift—her family—in service? When the pastor ended his sermon with, "How are you living your faith by serving others?" Heather felt convicted. "We have to do something besides taking care of one another," she said to herself—and to God.

After the service, the church offered a lunch of salad and sandwiches and encouraged people to visit the "missions fair." Heather and Jim had planned to take the kids for burgers after church and then drive to Jonas' Sunday afternoon soccer game. Marianne was planning to grab lunch at church and stay for youth choir practice; a friend's parents could drop her off at home. Heather said to Jim after the service, "Let's all just have lunch here and check out the missions fair really fast before we go to soccer."

While the children wolfed down lunch and she munched on a sandwich, Heather wandered among the twenty-some tables around the church fellowship hall, each with posters and brochures of various service opportunities in the community. Some were social service agencies that were asking for volunteers to teach English as a Second Language classes, to do chores for elderly adults who needed help if they were going to be able to stay in their own homes, to befriend a refugee family being resettled in their community, to be a mentor in a support program for impoverished single mothers who were attending a job readiness program at the community college. The boy scouts were there asking for leaders, and the elementary school was asking for tutors. Heather walked by all the tables and found herself stopping at one with a sign that said "Calvary Methodist Church Children's Recreation Program."

Around the sign were pictures of African American children playing basketball, sliding down a waterslide, playing Chutes and Ladders at a picnic table. Calvary Methodist was a small African American congregation in the poorest community of the city. The little church had ambitiously turned its corner parking lot into a safe place for the community's children to play. They had put up a fence to keep drug dealers out and bouncing balls in. They purchased play equipment and picnic tables. Now they were seeking volunteers who would help supervise and play with the children of their community. Thinking back to the moment, Heather said, "I was convicted, and I just said, 'We're doing this. This is something we can do together as a family.'"

It seemed easy enough. Calvary needed volunteers to show up for two hours one evening each week through the summer months and supervise the children, making sure they were safe and having fun. A smiling woman with a name badge proclaiming her to be Deena answered Heather's questions. "Yes," she said, "there will always be a head volunteer who can help you if you have a problem; she has access to Band-Aids and keys to the game closet." She was a little perplexed when Heather asked, "Can my whole family volunteer?" "We are really asking for adults who can supervise children," Deena replied. But Heather held her ground. "My husband and I'll volunteer, but I want to bring our kids with us. They can help with younger children." Deena turned the sign-up sheet toward Heather, and Heather signed them up for Tuesday evenings, beginning the Tuesday after Memorial Day.

Heather had not even consulted her family; she just knew that was what they needed to do. But after she had written "Heather and Jim Hall and children—Marianne, Jonas, and Sarah" on the Tuesday night sign-up sheet, she called Jim over to meet Deena, and to show him what she planned for them to do.

Jim laughed as he reflected back more than a year later on that Sunday afternoon. Heather often pushed him into doing things he would not do on his own. He certainly would not have chosen to spend an evening a week playing basketball and kickball on a black asphalt inner-city parking lot in the heat of the summer. He was still a bit incredulous. "If it was slightly outside her comfort zone, it's really outside my comfort zone. I'm busy; I didn't have time." Heather reflected back, "I was convicted, and I just said, 'We're doing it.' Suddenly, I was just going to make it happen."

That first Tuesday was more than a month after they had signed up, and in the weeks between the missions fair and their first foray into the Calvary community, Jim and Heather had second thoughts and misgivings. Jim said, "We'd known other friends who had volunteered there the summer before, so we were familiar with the program and the opportunity. But we had never ventured into that part of town. And we didn't know anyone else who had taken their children." Their church and Calvary had been partnering to serve in that community for more than ten years, but this was the Hall family's first involvement in that partnership. Ten years ago, Calvary had considered moving to the suburbs, but instead, a number of larger churches in the area had agreed to partner with Calvary to help them stay in the inner city and "make a difference" there. Jim described their own church as "a pretty typical suburban church—a lot of middle- and upper-class professionals; not a place that the folks around Calvary are going to come to. So our congregation decided to go to them." Even though they had never done anything like this before, even though they had never even visited Calvary's neighborhood, their congregation and friends had gone before them, and that pushed Heather and Jim to keep their commitment, even in the midst of their misgivings.

The only family member who really wanted to go on that first Tuesday was Sarah. She was excited to try out the playground. Marianne was quiet and withdrawn, her fifteen-year-old body language saying louder than any words could have communicated, "I don't want to go." Mom said to the silence in the car as they drove across town, "Look, if we don't want to, we don't have to go back after tonight, but let's just try it."

When they arrived, a young man wearing a bright blue T-shirt greeted them. "He gave all of us bright blue T-shirts, even us kids, that said 'Recreation Leader' on the back and 'Calvary Methodist Church' on the front. Like we needed identification—we were the only white kids there," Marianne remembered. Her dad added, "It was like, 'Here's your T-shirt; now, make a difference in these kids' lives.'" Calvary had actually prepared T-shirts in the sizes of their children.

As Sarah remembered that first evening, "When I got there the first time, I saw the monkey bars, and I really like those. So I just told my mom I was going over there to play. I met a couple of new friends and I started playing with them. Each time we went, I would meet new friends. One time there was this girl about my age, and she knew how to do double Dutch jump rope, so my mom and I did double Dutch with her."

Heather smiled at the memory. "I had thought we were doing this great thing for these poor kids, to give them a safe place to play. And then I realized, 'My kids need this. They need to have friends like this, who aren't all white and middle class and just like them.'" She was remembering holding one end of the jump rope for her daughter and her new friend.

Jim said, "You don't have to be experts at anything. If you can play Chutes and Ladders, then play Chutes and Ladders. If you can shoot a basketball, then shoot a basketball. You don't have to be Michael Jordan. You could just be there. I guess that a lot of the children there don't seem to get much individual attention from adults. Sometimes I'm just an extra set of hands to direct kids to the ladder for the slide, or another voice saying, 'Don't sit on the railing.' It wasn't hard—we just needed to show up and be there."

Show up they did. All summer Jim and Heather and their three children spent Tuesday evenings on Calvary's corner playground. Then they expanded their involvement to Saturdays, riding with the children in the church bus to the zoo or the swimming pool on Saturday morning. *Someone* went each Tuesday and each Saturday. Sometimes one parent or the other would take one of the children to some other responsibility. But most of the time all of the family went. The children loved it. They were not "helping"—they were playing with new friends. And as they drove to and from Calvary each week, they talked about the friends they were making, how their lives were alike and different, and what they were learning.

During the following winter, fifteen-year-old Marianne reflected on her family's summer volunteering. She told me that she thought it was "cool," because it was different from where she lives and goes to school, where almost everyone is white. She thought it was strange to be in the minority, to be friends with people who are a different color and who talk differently than her school classmates. "It opened my eyes," she said. "It made me thankful for everything I have, because, you know, I live in a safe community, and it was cool to give them a safe community where they could come and play, too." She admitted that sometimes she did not really want to go because it was summer, and there were other things that she wanted to do. "But then I would think, 'Well, it's only two hours on Tuesday evening and a Saturday morning, and I can give that to hang out with these kids.' So I think I learned not to be so selfish." She has grown up in a family that has always been involved in church. "I have always known about Jesus and we always pray and stuff, and so that's not new to me. But going to Calvary, I met kids from the neighborhood who had not participated in church life. I hope by the way I acted they could feel God's love."

In our conversation, Jim followed his daughter by commenting that they live in a community that is very "Christian"; there seems to be a church on almost every corner. "Missions always tended to be someplace out there—Africa—in our minds. This was just a small opportunity to try to connect in our own community and make a little bit of a difference."

Heather told me that her perspective has really changed on her church. "Before, I just thought about, 'Do my kids have a good Sunday school teacher?' Now, I'm thinking, 'It's okay that the programs for our kids are crowded, and that we're sometimes inconvenienced because there is a worship service in Spanish at the same time as ours, and they're using a bunch of rooms and some of the space.' Before, I would have looked at some of those activities and said, 'We can't even take care of our own, so why are we reaching out?' Now I know that's exactly what we should be doing. Inconvenient? If they bring their kids and the Sunday school classes are packed to overflowing, well, so what? That is exactly how it should be. It's not 'our' church. It's their church too!"

Jim remembered the first time they walked inside Calvary's playground fence, his family of five white people in the midst of a hundred African American children and adults. "We don't find ourselves in that situation very often," he understated. As the weeks went by, he reported that his wariness of the first few weeks turned to a deep sense of satisfaction; this was the right place for them. He remembers, "I no longer had a knot in the pit in my stomach when we walked in." And then he reflected on the fact that he would never have been there were it not for his wife. He reflected on the initial anxiety he felt working a setting more racially diverse than he had previously experienced. "A lot of people won't ever get past it if they're not presented with an opportunity like that."

There are other activities they could have engaged in as a middle-class family that would have been satisfying and yet felt "safer" because those activities would have kept the outside world at arm's length. Jim commented that they could have sponsored a child in Central America for $2.00 a day, and received pictures and letters to put on the refrigerator. But, he said, "the active participation can be a real catalyst; I'm not sure for what, but I know in the future, I'll look at opportunities to serve very differently." Jim and Heather are already planning to continue serving during the coming summer, maybe even two nights each week.

Heather went on to talk about how much she loved having the family all together for the evening at Calvary. It had become a priority for them, not just something to do if there wasn't a soccer game or a music lesson. "I loved watching my kids interact with the other kids. That was a delight. Seeing their world open up and then I realized that my world had opened up, too." She began by thinking that this was a good experience for her children—and then she realized it was good for her, too.

Jim agreed with her. It has changed his perspective. He feels part of the larger community now, a community with people who are somewhat different from him, and that is good for his family. He has felt racial barriers lowered that he had not even known were there. He has been surprised to realize that his values and priorities have changed. "If you had said to me two years ago that the church wanted to carve off $100,000 for English as a Second Language programming, because we have some community folks that can use our facilities and people in our church who can be instructors, I would have doubted that was something we really need to get involved in. Now I would say, 'Yes! That's a great way for us to be a better steward with what we've been given and engage in our surrounding community.' Everybody doesn't look like us and talk like us."

The Hall family still belongs to their suburban congregation, but they also consider themselves as belonging to Calvary and to the children and families of the Calvary community. The Hall family had just spent two hours on a weeknight and Saturday mornings playing with kids over a three-month period, less time than they usually spent watching their children play in the local soccer league, but it changed their understanding of their church, their community, their family, even their faith.

Why Families Start Serving Together

Even before they began serving in the recreation program at Calvary, the Hall family had a very busy family life: two full-time jobs and three very active children. What, then, moved them from thinking about what they "should" do to actually involve themselves not only in the beginning, but to continue weekly for months? Heather had been restless for some time, casting about and dissatisfied with the role of faith in their lives, seemingly just another of the many activity programs that engaged her family's "spare" time. She wanted their faith to be real and central in their lives.

For the Hall family, serving was not about plugging their fingers into one of the many gaping holes of need in the world around them. As an African American grandmother who volunteers in a free medical clinic said, "I do it because of the love of God, which is different than seeing a need and saying that I need to go do something about that." A single mom who works with her children to clean up the yards of elderly neighbors, serving in a homeless feeding program, and leading service projects with the youth group told me that they are living their beliefs by serving in the community.

These Christians are restless for their faith to mean something. Parents and grandparents feel compelled to make faith real in the lives of their children. I met a Methodist grandfather who serves lunch for homeless people every Saturday and takes his grandchildren with him because he wants them to learn to respect and value all kinds of people, and to learn "active faith." Heather and Jim talked about their joy in seeing their children make friends with African American children. Some adults begin serving because it is "good for the kids," or because they are humoring a spouse, only to find their own lives transformed.

Jonathan is a very successful lawyer who found himself dragged into working in an inner-city ministry with his wife, Grace. Grace had been volunteering there for some time, appointed to serve on the board of the ministry by their congregation. The more she learned about the ministry, the more she wanted to be involved. Then she roped Jonathan into teaching budgeting skills on Saturdays to families at risk for homelessness. She did not have to keep dragging him, however; he was soon hooked. He commented that working with the families at the ministry is a lot more meaningful for him than playing golf on Saturdays like the other lawyers in his firm. Over time, the family's involvement in the ministry has become the center of their lives together. Even their grown children who live independently join them on many Saturdays in the various programs of the community ministry center. Jonathan tried to explain why he keeps at it:

> We've got "stuff" to make us happy, but we want to get to the joy, and we've found what gives us joy. Happiness is like getting a new car. It smells new, and you drive it for a while and then it gets dirty, and it's not new anymore. It's nice, but it's not new and the happiness factor starts going down, and then to get back to happy again, you've got to get another new car. But joy is even after whatever it is that you're involved in is finished, there's something that resides in you. It makes you smile in the middle of the day and you can't think of anything in particular that's happening. It just clothes you.

These families were not motivated to serve because they thought they could meet the needs of the world. But they did see an opportunity to do something that would be genuinely helpful; the service they could provide made sense and might really help those they would serve. Heather was a mother who knew how important it was for children to have a safe place to play on summer evenings. Jonathan was a financially successful lawyer, restless with the trappings of his career and professionally acquainted with families pulled apart by financial difficulties. Their places of service made sense to them and to their families.

There are so many injustices in the world—poverty, epidemics, hunger, abused children—the list goes on until we have closed our ears and retreated to the safety of our homes, flipping television channels to escape the disasters that fill the news. We are overwhelmed—and consequently, immobilized. What can we do in the face of so much need? So many of us pray for God's intervention, but we personally find no handle where we can grab hold. These families had found handles, ways to express their faith in meaningful ways.

For many of the families we met, some catalyst had helped them make the connection between their restlessness to serve as an expression of their faith and a place that fit their calling, a catalyst such as the mission fair and the rallying sermon in Heather's congregation. Although the needs were not the initial stimulus for their involvement in service, the needs of others did give them direction and a place to begin. Heather's family can give children a safe place to play. They can be friends. They can meet and become friends with those children's parents. And together, perhaps the friendship and the safety offered reinforces community parents' attempts to keep their children away from the gangs and the drugs, to "make it."

A Home Full of Children

Susan and Mark Crismon are members of a Pentecostal church. They wanted children, but none ever came; they were busy with careers and just never got around to adoption, although they talked about it off and on. Five years ago, they built their dream home on the shores of a lake twenty minutes outside the city. Just before they moved, Susan began spending an afternoon each week tutoring first graders in reading in an elementary school in an impoverished neighborhood not far from the hospital where she worked as a nurse. She fell in love with the children. Soon, she was tutoring two and then three days a week, even after the move and the longer commute. Mark was vice president of a bank not far from the school, and he and Susan sometimes invited the children she was tutoring to go out for hamburgers with them after the tutoring, with their parents' permission.

Toward the end of the school year, Susan learned from the school principal that the first graders she was tutoring were reading above grade level, an amazing feat since half the first grade students in the school would probably not be promoted to second grade because of their low reading skills. Susan was hooked. "I realized I could definitely make an impact, so I kept at it."

During the second year of tutoring, Susan was at home one afternoon sitting on the deck, looking out over the lake, mesmerized by the reflections on the water. She then heard God ask her in the silence of that moment if she was happy. She laughed as she recalled saying out loud in response to the silent voice, "Yes, I am, God, so what do you want?" She then felt a strong sense that God wanted her to spend more time with the children, more time helping them with their schoolwork. She talked it over with Mark later that day, and they both agreed that she would quit her job so that she could spend more time tutoring. They could do without her income, and it was what she wanted more than anything.

They were driving home from church several months after she had moved to tutoring five days a week at the school, and Mark said, "This is going to sound weird, but I've got something to tell you." Staring down the road, not looking at her, he proceeded to tell her that he felt that God was telling him to sell their dream home and move. Silent only for a moment, Susan then laughed and responded, "God is telling me the same thing." Mark pulled the car over, turned and looked at Susan, and in the hug that followed, they said okay to God.

In the ensuing weeks, they sold their lakefront home and moved to the inner city, in the neighborhood of the school where Susan was tutoring. As Susan said, "We don't believe that we are doing anything exceptional; we believe that we're just doing what we are called to do." As extraordinary as this story is, the theme was repeated by other families who had been serving for years. Notice the "we" language. Susan and Mark experienced God calling *their family*, not just them as individuals, even though Susan was initially doing most of the work.

After they moved, a new chapter in their service began. The need to which they found themselves responding literally came in their front door. Just a week after they had moved to their new inner-city home, and before Susan had resumed tutoring at the school, they met the first grader who lived next door. Susan had seen him at the school, and he knew her name. The next afternoon, he knocked on the front door at about 3:00. When Susan answered, he said, "Hi, there's nobody home at my house; can I come in?" Susan learned that he came home to an empty house each day because his mother worked and his older brother did not get out of school for another hour. He did not like being home alone, and he asked Susan if he could do his homework at her kitchen table until his older brother came home from school. Over the following weeks, whenever Susan was home, there he came. By November, one of the boys she had tutored twice a week the year before asked if he could come, too. Susan agreed, but said, "Just you two. No more!"

Susan stopped going to the school to tutor. Instead, for the rest of the school year, the two boys spent a part of each afternoon after school in Susan's kitchen. That was five years before our conversation. Susan told me with a smile that one is now a fifth grader and the other is a fourth grader, and they are both doing very well in school. Those two boys were the beginning of what has become Susan's afterschool program for the children of their neighborhood. Now she has eight or ten children every day. Together, they fix a snack, talk, sometimes play a game, and then do their homework with Susan's encouraging guidance. As soon as he can get home from work, Mark pitches in to help.

Pondering Family Stories of Service

Few families would begin tutoring as a once-a-week service activity if they knew it would lead to selling their home and relocating to the inner city, or having one member quit a job to devote the majority of her time to a volunteer ministry. I doubt Susan and Mark could have ever imagined when she first tried out tutoring how their lives would be transformed. Nor should every family think that service will take over their lives, although it has been journey of joy for Susan and Mark. Volunteering can be as simple as collecting and delivering household goods to a family whose home is destroyed by fire, or being sure that elderly neighbors' lawns are mowed. Or it may be a voice in a quiet moment that shakes life to the very house foundations, as it did for Susan and Mark. There are different callings, and different seasons of family life and of faith.

For some of these family members, they first began serving because they were restless for their faith to matter more, to make a difference in their lives and the lives of others. For others, they were simply roped into something a family member was doing who said, "Come go with me." Over time, their service became not just something they do; it became who they are. Serving was not just one more "faith activity" like going to church and singing in the choir. It defined their life together; as Jonathan said, "It keeps us anchored in the 'real' world, in contrast with the upper-middle-class wealth of this neighborhood."

One characteristic that these dramatically differing stories of family service seem to have in common is a lack of formal guidance received from their congregations. Even the catalytic sermon and mission fair that was Heather's path into involving her family did not focus on *family* service; that was her own doing. Nevertheless, they had indeed found their way into a service that became a defining feature of their life together. Evidently, they are not exceptional. As we noted in chapter 1, the *majority* of the families surveyed with the Church Census are already engaged in service together in their communities. For those who want to live faith as a family through service, these families can encourage, just as the volunteer friends who had served at Calvary in summers past pointed the way for the Halls. Families do not necessarily wait for congregation leaders to have a vision for family ministry. The next chapter will suggest ways families can engage in ministry together, whether or not their congregations are on board with them. Perhaps they can then chart paths for others, who can say, "Did you hear what the Halls did last summer and how much they loved it?"

Being restless, wanting faith to count for more, is the beginning. Then comes finding a place to start. Heather had been casting about, looking for a foothold in making faith more central in her family's life, for months, maybe years. Then came the Sunday when the Scripture passage and the sermon grabbed her attention, and the opportunity that seemed to fit her family's gifts was right there on a folding table in the fellowship hall.

That is not to suggest that there is no role for congregational leaders in family service! For many of these families, it took a word from someone else to be the spark that got them started in service. Sometimes that came in a sermon, as it did for the Hall family. For others, a church leader or a friend pulled them into trying something new for their family. A sermon hit home, or someone specifically said, "Come go with me." For Jonathan's wife, it was asking her to serve on a board. In the following chapters, we will explore how congregation leaders can help families find their place of service and keep at it over time. We will look at how congregations can become communities with a culture of service.

4

Come, Go with Me

I have a closet full of fabric for the sewing projects I dream of, and I subscribe to quilting magazines. But I have not made a quilt in years. Buying fabrics is a start, but it does not make me a quilter. I love to plan such projects and gather all the tools and materials, but then I have to live with the guilt of not doing them. I am the same way about the importance of exercise and diet. I like to read about healthy eating, and I faithfully pay for a gym membership. If I do not actually get some exercise and eat healthily, however, I may know how to improve my health, but I surely will not be healthier. Christian faith is like making quilts and getting exercise and eating right—it is about doing. God will not be concerned on the last day with whether we worried about the hungry or the poor, or even if we could spout with dismay and righteous indignation statistics about the rates of poverty and the lack of food security in our world. God will be concerned with what we did about the needs of our neighbors, even when those needs seemed overwhelming and we wondered where we could possibly intervene that would actually do some lasting good. Surely the disciples, when confronted by a multitude of hungry people, were similarly overwhelmed and were sure there was nothing they could do in response that would really count for much of anything. They were out in the countryside, where a great crowd of people had followed Jesus:

> When he looked up and saw a large crowd coming toward him, Jesus said to Philip, "Where are we to buy bread for these people to eat?" He said this to test him, for he himself knew what he was going to do. Philip answered him, "Six months' wages would not buy enough bread for each of them to get a little."
>
> One of his disciples, Andrew, Simon Peter's brother, said to him, "There is a boy here who has five barley loaves and two fish, but what are they among so many people?" Jesus said, "Make the people sit down." Now there was a great deal of grass in that place; so they sat down, about five thousand in all. Then Jesus took the loaves, and when he had given thanks, he distributed them to those who were seated; so also the fish, as much as they wanted. When they were satisfied, he told his disciples, "Gather up the fragments left over so that nothing may be lost." So they gathered them up, and from the fragments of the five barley loaves, left by those who had eaten, they filled twelve baskets. When the people saw the sign that he had done, they began to say, "This is indeed the prophet who is to come into the world." (John 6:5-14)

I can only imagine the dismay the disciples felt when Jesus told them to feed more than five thousand people. How could their inadequate resources possibly matter in the face of thousands of people? When Jesus asked the disciples how they planned to address the need in front of them, Jesus already knew what *he* was going to do. He asked what *they* were going to do to *teach* them, to *test* them. As a teacher, I always mean for tests to be opportunities for learning. I doubt my students see the learning in the test; they think the learning comes in the preparation. Perhaps it does, but often it is when we attempt to answer problems that we actually learn the lessons. Preparing can only take us so far. This feeding of the thousands of people on that hillside—with a boy's lunch box equivalent of a tuna fish sandwich—was Jesus teaching the disciples.

Jesus often used children to teach adults. People were hungry, and it was late, and this little boy simply offered what he had, as insufficient as it was, in the face of the need before them all. It was up to Jesus, then, to bless and multiply the loaves, which he did. Most of us have seen a child put a coin in an offering plate or give a beloved possession as an impulsive self-sacrifice to help another child in need. One family I interviewed who had been engaged in a ministry of providing blankets and clothing to homeless people in their city began their work when their son carried the blanket from his own bed to his dad. He had heard on the evening news that it was going to be a record-setting cold night and city officials were attempting to open temporary shelters for those who were otherwise at risk for freezing. The son had seen homeless people under the overpass on the way to his school. "Please, Dad, let's go give my blanket to one of those guys we see when we go to school in the mornings." What is one blanket in the face of the needs of scores of homeless people on a freezing night?

Such actions touch us. We may even call such a seemingly small gesture "cute." In so doing, we diminish the profound act of giving whatever one has. "Cute" usually means smaller than the norm but nice, as in, "The apartment has a cute kitchen." If there is one thing a child's giving is *not*, however, it is small. The size of a gift is not the extent to which it fits some need "out there," but rather the proportion of what one has that the gift represents. Jesus sat in the temple and watched people putting their gifts into the treasury. Rich people put in large amounts, but when a poor widow put in two coins worth less than a penny, Jesus counted it more than the large gifts of the wealthy, saying, "For all of them have contributed out of their abundance; but she out of her poverty, has put in everything she had, all she had to live on" (Mark 12:44). The problem is that we have heard this so many times that it has lost its surprise. But think about it; we are called to serve and our service is not to be measured by the extent to which we address the need before us, but rather by the extent to which we truly give ourselves completely in service to others.

Such giving is a sign of the kingdom of God. When we serve others, we all hope and pray that God will use us for healing and for hope and for changing lives. Ultimately, however, that is God's business. We are not called to be effective change agents in the world—we are called to be faithful servants, faithful children offering whatever we have to share with others. And when we do so, *we* are changed. When we serve, we will meet God in the faces of the poor and the immigrant and the child we tutor—whomever it is that we give our hands and hearts and blankets and tuna fish sandwiches. We will meet God there just as surely as Stephen met God in the faces of the Greek widows he served.

Jesus expected his followers to give whatever resources they had, and when the boy responded with his supper, Jesus blessed it so that it was enough and more. Psalm 147 says that our God is a God who is continuing to create stars and name each one, whose understanding and power are so vast we cannot begin to comprehend. But that same powerful, star-creating God is also and at the same time the God who bandages our wounds and our broken hearts. The God we worship is active, is doing—from creating celestial bodies to putting Band-Aids on the cuts and scrapes of God's children—and taking our willingness to give what we have and miraculously multiplying into sufficiency and even wealth beyond need, baskets full of overflow.

Because we belong to God, that psalm also says who we are. We cannot create celestial bodies; we cannot heal the hurts and injustices of God's children. But we can celebrate the beauty of God's creation. Moreover, we can actively offer what we have. We can bring the bandages and tuna fish sandwiches and love through which *God* can heal and feed God's children in miraculous ways. By caring for those hurt or cast out by a society that sees them as insignificant and expendable, we participate in the work of this mighty God. This God is creating the universe—flinging the stars in space—and at the same time, keeping track of even the sparrows and the hairs on our heads.

The families I interviewed had learned the freedom of simply giving what they have. The Halls had learned that. Their loaves and fishes were their faithfulness to show up, willing to hold a jump rope or shoot baskets or play Chutes and Ladders. Toby pushed a lawn mower back and forth across neighbors' lawns; his dad drove neighbors to the doctor and paid their utility bills; his mom collected household goods for a family who lost everything in a house fire. The Crismons had learned that. They gave their time and love of children and ended up with a life far richer than they had dreamed. There is a wonderful freedom in recognizing that our families are only called to serve in ways that we are able, using the resources we have.

Starting Where You Are

Of course, the only gift we can give is what we have; and the only place we can begin is where we find ourselves. We certainly cannot give what we do not have or begin where we are not! Perhaps that sounds simplistic, but it is important focus that comes with attention to serving as an expression of faith rather than because of the world of need all around us. The needy world tends to paralyze us with inadequacy; our faith, on the other hand, motivates and mobilizes.

You are probably already engaged in service to others in one way or another. If you are, how can you bring your family alongside to join you? Perhaps there is an issue that concerns you deeply: children struggling in school, families burdened with caring for a parent with Alzheimer's disease, children who are behind in school because their parents cannot read English and help them with homework, the misuse of the glorious created world God told us to be responsible for—the list is as long as the world is big. God does not call us to serve in places we are not or for causes we do not care much about. God's calling is to those things that set our hearts on fire.

Sometimes the start of family serving comes from something besides a sense of calling or determination to put action to faith, however. For me, it came out of a worry about one of my children. I told the story in this book's introduction of my concern that our family was not nourishing the faith of our daughter, and so we found ourselves serving in a program for homeless families.

The opportunities for service are all around us, but they may not look like opportunities for families, particularly families with young children. Be persistent, though, and remember that even if your family just has two pennies worth of time or skills to offer, that is exactly what you are called to give. If you do not know where to begin, talk to a religious leader or a professional social worker in your congregation about what you would like to do, and ask them to help you find a place to plug in. It may be adopting a senior adult in assisted living or a nursing facility to visit once a week as a family, or volunteering together in an inner-city agency. Be stubborn about wanting to be involved in a way that enables your family to know those on the receiving end of the services, and they will have opportunity to know you.

Moving from "My" Project to "Our" Project

We learned from the families that we interviewed that community service usually begins with the engagement of one family member, who then recruits the rest of the family. Someone serves as the catalyst. In our family, I called the shelter to find out what we could do, and then I said, "Let's go." Someone has to take the initiative. For many families, the service evolves over time, sometimes involving additional family members or becoming a different kind of involvement than at the start.

For example, Maria and Jose Rodriquez deliver food to homebound seniors each week. As they formed relationships over time with people to whom they carried lunch, they asked about their birthdays and began baking birthday cakes and bringing birthday parties with lunch. They visited one of the women on their route when she was hospitalized. When one of the recipients died, the couple prepared the food for the after-funeral gathering of family members from out of town. What began as a once-a-week meals-on-wheels route has become a much broader involvement in the lives of those they serve.

Mark Crismon, whose wife, Susan, runs the afterschool program in their home for the neighborhood children, volunteers to help the children's single mothers when they have home maintenance jobs they do not know how to do on their own. He began taking his vacation in the summer in half days so that he could help his wife with the children during the summer months when school is out. He said, "The more I do, the more my eyes and ears find other opportunities to care for these neighbors."

Not only does the ministry change over time, but the family may also pull others into their shared work. Beth is a single mom; she and her children volunteered in an inner-city tutoring program. Soon after starting there, she had talked her sister into joining her every Tuesday. Her sister was several years older and had just moved back to the community after being away for years, at least in part because of family conflict and hurt that led to estrangement between the sisters. As they worked together in the tutoring program and talked about the children they grew to love, the hurt that had driven them apart began to dissolve, and Beth's children developed a relationship with an aunt that they had barely known before.

I also learned that there is no one way to be a family service team; there are probably as many different variations as there are families serving together. Some families have one service "leader" and the others "help out." Sometimes one is more involved than others, but others join in when they can. Some are equal partners and do everything together. Others show up together and then divide up and "do their own thing," but they talk about their service beforehand and afterward, and they see it as "our" work. Just as it is in much of our lives as families, about the time you figure out who is in what role, it will probably change.

For example, it was Maria who first started taking lunches to homebound senior adults. When Jose retired, she talked him into driving. They enjoy talking as they ride together, and she feels safe going into the homes of the people they serve with him along. Therefore, they are forming stronger relationships with those who are homebound. One day, they had their preschool grandson Tory for the day, so they just put Tory's infant car seat in the car and took him with them to deliver meals. It was such a great experience for Tory and his grandparents and the persons to whom they deliver food that Tory often goes with them now. Tory loves to help carry the food to the door, and everyone is always delighted with his presence. Tory is learning to serve at the same time he is learning to walk.

Serving as a team helps family members stay involved when they might not if they were serving as individuals. Jose explained, "Sometimes I get tired, and I just want to slip back, but she's depending on me. I say to myself, 'I'm not going to quit because I'll hold her back. I need to keep going and keep strong.'" Jim Hall talked about his temptation to quit the weekly recreational program. They have very busy lives, with three children involved in all the activities that other suburban children are engaged in—sports teams and music lesson and church groups. Jim knew that if it had been up to him, he would have come up with some excuse to bail out. He stuck with it, though, because it was not just him—it was a commitment he had made to his family and a commitment they had made together.

Of course, adults are not the only ones who are tempted to quit, but the family keeps them keeping on. One family committed themselves to rising before dawn every Saturday to prepare lunch for the people in a homeless shelter. They have not looked back; it is a "we" commitment. The mother of the family said of her sixteen-year-old son, "Maybe as Michael gets a little older, he would rather stay in the bed at 5:00 on Saturday morning instead of go out, but I give him a little shove, and then he's up." How many sixteen-year-old boys—or thirty-six-year-old adults, for that matter—voluntarily get up at 5:00 a.m. on Saturdays to help cook for hungry people? Perhaps there would be many more if we served together.

Individual volunteering is very different than family volunteering—even if family members go together. To illustrate, one father talked about his involvement in a community service organization. He has told the family they are welcome to come, with the challenge, "If they want to be with me, they'll go with me." Wife and daughter can choose to go with him, or not. It is *his* activity. Some of the volunteers told us that, unlike family service, individual projects can actually be a strain on family life, pulling family members away from one another rather than together in shared activity.

Serving People, Not Projects

There are many opportunities to volunteer that include raising money, cleaning up neighborhoods, painting, or stuffing envelopes. Such projects can be a great place to start, but the most meaningful activities are those in which families can meet and know those they serve. Similarly, a family picking up litter in a park together as a way of caring for God's created world is a helpful companion activity to giving money to organizations that care for creation. Caring for a park together becomes even more meaningful if a family serves alongside neighborhood residents who share the park. Giving money is important, but it does not deepen faith and a sense of calling as a family unless rooted also in personal interaction with a real green space and its creatures, including its humans.

Visiting a social service program or doing a one-shot service project can be a great way to get a family's feet wet. Such a project can include serving a holiday meal in an inner-city feeding program, delivering Christmas cookies in a nursing home, or working in a congregation-sponsored "toy store," with donated toys available at deeply discounted prices for low-income parents to buy for their children for Christmas. Such opportunities can be real eye-openers for both children and adults; we learn about lives that may be very different from our own, and we learn about ourselves in noticing our reactions to the experience. The real outcome of such projects truly is the education of those serving and learning about what kinds of involvement are best aligned with our gifts and calling.

It is better for a family to start with a small beginning that they can build on, rather than to promise more than they can really do and then end up feeling that they have let others down and failed. Families may need reminding that they are called to serve as a way of living their faith, not because they can single-handedly fix all the world's problems. Not all service needs to be ongoing or time-intensive. A family spending a couple of hours on a Saturday morning raking leaves and mowing grass for an elderly neighbor can be a very meaningful service activity. Adopting a shut-in senior adult and visiting with a plate of fruit or homemade cookies for thirty minutes once a week can be a significant experience for both the senior and the adoptive family. Such limited commitments may then lead to greater involvement.

When God had completed the creation, God declared a day of rest and paused to look over all that had been created. In the same way, families need to make time, even if it is in the car on the way home, to reflect on the work they did together, remembering together why serving is important to them. Families need to talk with one another and with God about their experience. Service is often rewarding in itself, but nevertheless celebration is a great way to frame the work together. Such a frame can be stopping for ice cream, or a romp or walk in the park, or popping popcorn and playing a favorite game together that evening. If service is an expression of faith, then celebrating that service is important.

Celebrating and remembering why we serve are especially important when the service is less than satisfying. Sometimes those served may not be as grateful for the family's work as we think they should be. We may be able to see clearly the ways that those served could change their circumstances for the better, but they keep on keeping on in what look like dead-end life patterns. We may clean up a park on Saturday afternoon, only to find somebody trashed it on Saturday night. It can help families to work alongside others who are also trying to live out their own understanding of the gospel in visible commitments to service. It helps to have others with whom to share successes and disappointments and unanticipated learning with. Chapter 6 provides guidance for congregational leaders who want to develop a congregational culture of service. That leader could be you.

Facing the Challenges

There will be challenges.[1] The families we interviewed talked about the challenges they had experienced. Several said that people important to them did not understand or support their service. Some families sensed that their service came with risks. Many struggled to find time to serve. Finally, several described unexpected changes they experienced in themselves. Knowing that these challenges are common may not help families and religious leaders avoid them so much as keep the challenges in perspective with the overall impact of service on family life.

People Important to You May Not Understand

Sometimes friends and family may not just misunderstand but be actively critical of the service commitments a family makes. Susan Crismon's mother did not like their move to the inner city and refused to come for a visit when there were African American children in Susan's home. Susan chose to continue caring for the children, resulting in distancing from her mother. Others may not say anything, but a silent disapproval may hang in the air. Moreover, service takes time, and sometimes that may mean less time to spend with friends and extended family. Even if the relationships continue, they may change. One young couple I interviewed had intentionally moved into an inner-city neighborhood to be of service there. Their friends come to visit, but they all live in the suburbs, and over time, the spaces of time between their gatherings have gradually become longer and longer.

Service Has Real Risks

For many of the families we interviewed, volunteering meant that they had to do something they had never done before in a place and/or with people that were at least initially strange to them—and to which they were exposing the persons they love the most. Several families described the initial experience as "going beyond our comfort zone." Most learned to feel safe in a neighborhood that had formerly made them wary; they felt competent to provide the service they were providing; they had found a place for themselves in this new environment. Nevertheless, we live in a violent world. Serving people in difficult circumstances can sometimes involve real risks that need to be understood. Heather and Jim knew that there were drug dealers in the neighborhood where they took their children to the recreational program to serve, and they made rules about coming and going, about who to trust and who not to trust. Susan and Mark Crismon knew that there were robberies in the neighborhood to which they were moving. They put strong locks on their doors and windows and installed an outdoor safety lighting system. Jose and Maria realized that, although they felt safe with the persons to whom they delivered meals, the neighborhoods were not always safe. They always went together and kept a cell phone with them. Jesus taught us as we go where he sends us to be "wise as serpents and innocent as doves" (Matt 10:16).

It Is a Struggle to Find the Time

It is no news that finding the time to serve is a challenge. The families we interviewed struggled to add significant blocks of service time to already busy calendars. They learned to set boundaries on what they could do and what they could not. On the other hand, serving together actually becomes a time for the family to be together. They were struggling, but they were struggling well and they were committed to the struggle because serving was important to them.

Your Family and Your Worldview Will Change

All of these families talked about the transformation that took place in themselves, more even than in those they served. Susan Crismon talked about learning to see herself differently, as the children saw her, and it was unsettling. One afternoon, one of the little boys who spends afternoons in her home looked up at her during snack time and asked, "Mrs. Crismon, are you white or are you mixed?" She asked him what he thought, and he replied, "I think you must be mixed because you don't act like a white person." She realized that these young children had ideas about white society and black society that she knew little about. She said sadly, "I didn't know the barriers were as strong as they seem to be."

Jonathan Matthews is the lawyer who initially became involved in the community ministry by providing a budgeting class for families at risk of homelessness. Jonathan told me that he had been changed by learning to "see the world through the eyes of a child from that community." He talked about volunteers who come to help for an event, such as an Easter egg hunt or a Christmas party. "They leave feeling good about having served." In fact, the center intentionally provides such opportunities for one-time volunteers to experience the community ministry center's work. Working there day in and day out as he and his family do, however, is different; "because you see the good parts, and you see the bad parts, and you see the happy and the sad, and it's all mixed together just like your own family."

It is that "all mixed together" complexity that is "just like us." This learning took a long time in coming. Jonathan and his wife noted that relationships with community residents did not just form overnight; it had taken six years before people in the neighborhood started really "leveling" with them, realizing that they are there "for good," not just for one-shot, feel-good projects.

Families spoke of having their eyes opened to a different reality than they had known, of the challenges the service recipients face on a daily basis. Jonathan went on to say that he had been so naïve before he began his involvement in an impoverished community. The neighborhood was littered with trash; there were old tires and open trash bags strewn over abandoned lots. He remembers thinking that people were just trashy, that they just did not care what the neighborhood looked like.

As he began to make friends in the community and spent more time there, however, he learned that the city trash pickup is spotty and irregular, unlike the clockwork city pickup service in his own upper-middle-class neighborhood. He said, "I had just never thought about it. If there's a neighborhood that has trash around, then trash begets trash." He learned that building contractors had figured out that instead of paying money to dispose of trash from their worksites, they could just dump it in this neighborhood. "People come in and dump, actually dump trash in the neighborhood because there is trash around."

When his wife first cajoled him into serving with her, he had no idea that the community ministry would become so central to their lives, would even change the focus of his career—all because of what he learned about his city's relative neglect of this poor, "trashy" community. He began to realize what Micah 6:8 meant for him.

Seeking Justice, Loving Kindness, Walking with God

Micah 6:8 calls us to do justice, to love kindness, to walk in humility with God, and family service results in plenty of opportunity to live all three aspects of that calling.

Seeking Justice

As we care for people, we begin to realize that it would be so much better if we could change the systems that cause the needs that we are trying to address. By all means, we should be feeding people who are homeless. But as we feed them, we begin to ask why they are homeless and hungry in the first place. We all know the saying that if you give a man a fish today, he will be hungry tomorrow;

but if you teach him how to fish, he can feed himself for all his tomorrows. There may be more to the problem than simply that he has no fishing skills, however. What if he has no access to a pond where he can fish; what if the shoreline is all owned by hotels and rich folks? Can we figure out ways to get him the right to go fishing? Perhaps we can give him a financial boost to help him buy his own fishing pole, and then perhaps his own pond. Then we need to think further; perhaps he needs a truck to drive the fish to market and support his whole family with profit from his catch.

As my children patiently tutored that little boy trying to catch up in school despite his hearing loss from those untreated ear infections, we became advocates for health care for all children regardless of income. Would it not have been so much better if we could have intervened earlier and saved his hearing? And what if we had pushed our city to provide public transportation to that area of town where people most needed it? Perhaps we could have helped to develop a job training program that paid participants so that they could support their families while they learned job skills—so his daddy could learn a trade instead of going from one day labor job to another.

The Hebrew word *tzedakah* that is translated as "righteousness" or "justice" has to do with treating poor individuals justly. In its highest form, justice means enabling them to rise above poverty and remain there. Justice has a different focus than charity, which meets a present need. Charity focuses on meeting the need for today—feeding a hungry person. Justice focuses on tackling the forces that created the need in the first place.

Back to Jonathan, the lawyer serving with his wife on Saturdays in a community ministry in the poor part of town. Jonathan began to realize that it was not that the people in the community where they were serving were "trashy," but that contractors were dumping construction trash in the community, and that the city was not providing regular trash pickup—and trash begets trash. So, Jonathan used his very effective skills as a lawyer to lean on the city to increase the trash pickup in the area. As they cleaned up the parks, the neighbors cleaned up their yards, and a new sense of pride washed over the community. The city replaced the streetlights, and mothers were more willing to trust the neighborhood and allow their children to play outdoors. And Jonathan's legal career began to shift toward legal advocacy for impoverished communities in their city.

We are not responsible for bringing in the kingdom of God—that is God's business. But we can work toward justice for people who are in our circle of concern, and in doing so, paint a picture of the justice of God that will come with that kingdom. We can *live into* "thy kingdom come, thy will be done." Over and over, the Bible calls us to do justice, to minister not only to the needs of persons who have been hurt by society's injustice, but to speak out against unjust systems themselves.

Loving Kindness

The families we interviewed who were active in their communities also were open to folding others into their life together, sometimes as family members. Adopted children in one family asked their parents if they could "adopt" a senior adult couple as their grandparents, which they all agreed to do. One woman said that they tend to collect "strays," people alone in the world. "We just have them come and be a part of our family." Mark Crismon, whose wife runs the afterschool program in their home, said, "We've acquired all these grandchildren; we just fell in love with them. They are our kids."

That is not to say that service is all about sweetness and group hugs. The permeable boundaries are sometimes a source of frustration and tension. People get tired and on one another's nerves. Susan Crismon quipped, "It would be wonderful if I were perky all the time, but there are days when 6:00 hits and I can't wait for those kids to go home. I just turn off all the lights and just lie on the bed and just stare into space."

Even so, they keep on keeping on. Although being involved in family service for at least a year was the benchmark for being included in the study, in fact, these families had been involved far longer—ten years, twenty years, more than thirty years. Parents said they want to pass their commitment to service to the next generation. As Lisa said, "All I wanted my boys ever to do was to care about other people, not to be so self-centered, but to care that there is somebody else out there that may be hurting." Loving kindness, serving, has become a core identity for some of these families. Their life together has been shaped by their service, from relocating to actually living in the community where they serve to spending vacations engaged in service projects. It is who they are.

A young husband married just three years said, "Because we serve together we have a common goal other than just making eyes at each other and loving each other and cooking dinner for each other." He thinks it has helped their marriage a lot to have a shared focus, that their life as a couple matters to others. Susan Crismon does not stay lying across the bed. The commitment she has made to the children of her neighborhood pulls her up and into another day: "I've tied loyalty and faithfulness around my neck and I've written it on my heart that I'm going to be here for these children and I think that's pleasing to God and that's what he's asked of me, just my little bundle of responsibility, as the Quakers used to say."

Walking Humbly with God

Even when we stay clear that we are serving as an expression of our faith, with no illusion that we are going to solve all the problems of the world, service still exposes us to those problems in in-our-face ways. We encounter the dragons that breathe fire and destruction into the lives of those we learn to care about, dragons such as poverty, homelessness, school failure, substance abuse, and HIV/AIDS. We really can identify with the widow who dropped two small copper coins in the offering in front of Jesus (Mark 12:42), or the boy David in the face of Goliath (1 Sam 17:40), or the little boy who offered his sack lunch to Jesus to help feed the thousands (John 6:9). We, too, have only two cents, five stones and a slingshot, bread buns and a can of tuna. Unless we abide in the love and promises of our Savior, we can do nothing. We know, however, that in the hands of the Lord such flimsy resources can lead to miracles. We have been promised that if we abide in Christ, if we keep our hand in His, our work will be fruitful; "ask for whatever you wish, and it will be done for you" (John 15:1-7). Whatever else we do, our doing justice and our loving kindness must be the fruit of our walk with God, and must be accompanied by our prayers for God's leadership and presence in our families' doing and loving:

> Do not worry about anything, but in everything by prayer and supplication with thanksgiving, let your requests be made known to God. And the peace of God, which surpasses all understanding, will guard your hearts and your minds in Christ Jesus. Finally, beloved, whatever is true, whatever is honorable, whatever is just, whatever is pure, whatever is pleasing, whatever is commendable—if there is any excellence and if there is anything worthy of praise—think about these things. I can do all things through him who strengthens me. (Phil 4:6-8, 13)

5

Remembering Why We Serve

On one occasion an expert in the law stood up to test Jesus. "Teacher," he asked, "what must I do to inherit eternal life?"

"What is written in the Law?" he replied. "How do you read it?"

He answered: "'Love the Lord your God with all your heart and with all your soul and with all your strength and with all your mind'; and, 'Love your neighbor as yourself.'"

"You have answered correctly," Jesus replied. "Do this and you will live."

But he wanted to justify himself, so he asked Jesus, "And who is my neighbor?"

In reply Jesus said: "A man was going down from Jerusalem to Jericho, when he fell into the hands of robbers. They stripped him of his clothes, beat him and went away, leaving him half dead. A priest happened to be going down the same road, and when he saw the man, he passed by on the other side. So too, a Levite, when he came to the place and saw him, passed by on the other *side. But a Samaritan, as he traveled, came where the man was; and when he saw him, he took pity on him. He went to him and bandaged his wounds, pouring on oil and wine. Then he put the man on his own donkey, took him to an inn and took care of him. The next day he took out two silver coins and gave them to the innkeeper. 'Look after him,' he said, 'and when I return, I will reimburse you for any extra expense you may have.'*

"Which of these three do you think was a neighbor to the man who fell into the hands of robbers?"

The expert in the law replied, "The one who had mercy on him."

Jesus told him, "Go and do likewise."

(Luke 10:25-37 NIV)

Who Is Our Neighbor?

The expert in the law who asked the question was hostile, challenging and testing Jesus. He wanted to make himself look good, presumably at Jesus' expense. This was not a genuine question—"Who is my neighbor?" This lawyer was asking, "Theoretically, Jesus, what do you mean when you say love your neighbor as yourself?" It is not entirely clear how the lawyer planned to trap Jesus with this question. Whatever the lawyer's intent, however, Jesus uses the opportunity to tell a powerful story that turns the lawyer's question on its head. It is a story that haunts us. Good stories do that; they leave us pondering.

After telling the story of the beat-up traveler in response to the question, "Who is my neighbor?" Jesus asks instead, "Who is a neighbor to this man?" If the lawyer's question had been applied to this story, he would have asked in which category the wounded traveler fit—"neighbor" or "not neighbor." Jesus' story obliterates that distinction. Instead, Jesus' question is, "Who chooses to *be* a neighbor to the traveler?" Mr. Rogers, the children's show celebrity, captures Jesus' question in his song, "Won't you be my neighbor?"[1] The question "who is neighbor" is about us, not about any group we call "them." We are called not to try to figure out who is and is not our neighbor, but to *be* a neighbor. We live in a world full of people who are singing Mr. Rogers' song to us.

Jesus' story is about a victim of highway robbery. We have to stretch to understand a story about going on a journey by walking miles and miles through a wilderness. In our world, such a trip would be taken in less than an hour zipping along at sixty miles per hour in a car. For those listening to Jesus, however, trips were made by walking, perhaps leading a pack animal who carried the luggage. The road from Jerusalem to Jericho was a long downhill trek from a plateau in the Judean mountains twenty-five hundred feet above sea level to the lowlands of the Dead Sea, which is almost fourteen hundred feet below sea level.[2] The rocky path led through a desolate, dry landscape without trees—just rocks and brush and no roadside amenities. Even today, there are still few signs of civilization along the way. Robbers routinely hid in the rocks along the path and ambushed travelers stupid enough to be out there alone. People who traveled this road normally did so in caravans to provide one another the safety found in numbers. The victim in Jesus' parable was foolish to travel alone; he certainly should have known better. But Jesus says nothing about the fact that his being robbed and injured was in large part due to his own foolhardiness.

Most of us know that many of our messes are at least in part our own creations. The issue is not whose fault it is that the man got robbed, although you can almost hear his mother saying, "What were you thinking, to be out there alone, just asking for trouble?" The point Jesus was trying to make was that the questions of whether or not the man was worthy of help or would learn from this experience were irrelevant. What is significant in the story are the attitudes of the potential helpers.[3] God expects us to respond to the needs of anyone who is on the same road with us—*anyone*. It is so easy to slip into thinking that we should minister only to those who are in trouble through no fault of their own and those who will responsibly use what help we provide. But Jesus made no such restriction for helping people.

Many of the folks with whom we serve are like the traveler. We can see more clearly, and perhaps they can in retrospect, that their troubles are of their own making. For Jesus, that is not the point. He also warned not to judge lest we be judged and to use the same measuring stick on ourselves that we use for others (Matt 7:1-5). They need help, and we are called to be neighbor—period. Moreover, those we serve not only often cause their own troubles, but they are not always grateful for our help nor do they necessarily change their ways. Jesus' story says nothing about the traveler saying "thank you" or resolving never to travel alone again. What calls us to be neighbor is not the others' capacity for seeing the error of their ways and making significant life changes. The saying "God helps those who help themselves" is not in the Bible.

In short, we cannot expect the people we serve to be grateful for our presence in their lives; when they are, that is gravy on the biscuit. If you are from the North, perhaps the saying for you is, "that's icing on the cake." That is, gratitude from those served is a delightful extra, but not the necessary bread (biscuit) that sustains us. That which sustains our service is the bread, the Bread of Life, the Jesus who calls us to see all persons in need as our "neighbor." People who are struggling with life can be depressed, whiny, angry, and unreliable. You may work hard to clear your schedule to serve, and the people you serve are not the least bit grateful for the sacrifice you have made. It may have been the acrobatic feat of the century to get your family together and organized to show up, and those you are supposed to be serving do not seem to appreciate your effort.

We want people to be grateful, at the very least, for what we do for them. In fact, we want more than gratitude from them. We want them to use our service as the inspiration to muster all their resources and pull themselves out of their problematic situation. We want to be the noble rescuers. I really hoped that the family we befriended would use our friendship and support to get job training so that the mom and dad could find steady employment. Then surely they could settle into the community and not have to rip their children out of school yet another time to follow seasonal employment. Heather and Jim and their children would love to know that the children in that summer recreational program would do better in school and avoid gang involvement because their family spent time each week with them. Would that not be wonderful payback for these gracious people who are pouring their energies into service?

As wonderful as it is when lives are changed and friendships are formed, the fundamental reason we serve is because Jesus tells us they are our neighbors. We do not serve contingent on those we serve being grateful or changing their lives. If we did, when others fail to change or even to be grateful for our service, we would just quit. We serve because that is how we show our love for God. Jesus did not finish the story the way we want, with the traveler expressing gratitude to his rescuer and vowing never to travel alone again. The story is finished—it is finished with the Samaritan's response.

Since God never stops loving us, then neither should we stop loving our neighbors. End of story. It is that simple, that glorious, and that hard. Of course, we do not serve without hope that our service will make a difference in people's lives. We ache to be used as instruments of healing and hope and opportunity for new beginnings to the people we serve. We try to give them our very best efforts. If people's lives do change, however, we give God the glory, because that is God's business. If through our faithful service, God uses us in the transformation of those we serve, then we thank God for that blessing—and laugh about the fact that God used us, little boys with bread and tuna fish in the face of a multitude. We simply give what we have; the miracle is up to God.

Rick Rusaw and Eric Swanson have suggested that we are like the young donkey that carried Jesus for his grand entrance into Jerusalem on what has become known as Palm Sunday (Matt 21:1-9).[4] Can you imagine what the donkey was thinking? Of all the donkeys, he was chosen to lead this parade. People were shouting, laying their clothes on the road for the donkey to clip clop across, waving tree branches and softening his path with them as well. Perhaps the donkey thought it was all about him. He was the one doing most of the work and at the center of all the activity that morning, after all. We, like the donkey, may be working hard, but it is not about us. The "crowd" responds to what we bring to them, whether with appreciation or indifference, not to us. We are not the focus of this ticker-tape parade. Nevertheless, it is surely a gift from God that we can be chosen to play the donkey part in the good news story in people's lives.

In the last chapter, we explored the story of the miraculous picnic on the hillside. Later in the evening of that same day, after Jesus multiplied the loaves and fishes for the thousands of people who had come to hear him teach, the disciples went on ahead of Jesus. He caught up with them by walking to them across the water, and then their boat was amazingly delivered from the strong wind and rough waters to the distant shore (John 6:16-21). All in all, it had been quite a miraculous day. The next morning, here came the crowds, looking for Jesus, looking for the miracle worker. When they found him, they asked for the gift he had displayed. "What must we do to perform the works of God?" they asked:

> Jesus answered them, "This is the work of God, that you believe in
> him whom he has sent." So they said to him, "What sign are you
> going to give us then, so that we may see it and believe you? What
> work are you performing?" (John 6:29-30)

It had been less than twenty-four hours since the crowd had eaten their fill in the wilderness banquet begun by a boy sharing his sack lunch. They were guessing that somehow Jesus had done something unusual, even miraculous, to get to the other side of the lake, because they saw the disciples go ahead without him. Most likely, the disciples had talked about the Lord walking on the water, and that story had spread rapidly. So here they were, asking for a sign. How could they keep asking Jesus for more evidence? Had they not seen enough? It is even more telling that they ask Jesus to show them how he did it so they can do miracles, too.

When we expect our service to be met with changed lives and restored hopes, then we are like that Galilean crowd, asking to know how to perform the "works of God." We want to be the workers of miracles in the lives and communities where we serve. That would confirm for us that our service is really God's work. Is this what we are supposed to be doing? Is God with us? Is our work with the poor and troubled children and persons with all kinds of life challenges really blessed? We want to *see* God at work and long for concrete signs of eternal significance. Like the crowd, bread for today is not enough for us. We want more than simple sustenance. We want a hold on that which will last, even which is eternal. We want to *contribute* to it, to be about God's work. Is that so unreasonable?

Jesus responds that the work of God is belief in the one God has sent. He goes on to tell us that if we come to him, we will never be hungry; if we believe in him, we will never be thirsty (v. 35). In other words, we cannot put our trust in that which we can see, much less in what we can accomplish by our own efforts. Our work is to flow from our belief, our trust in Jesus the Christ, and not the other way around. To trust Jesus means to live out his command to put the littlest first. But our energy and security in what we are doing does not come from the response of those served. Our compassion and commitment come from the one who sustains us, who calls us to serve, who meets us and walks with us in the work we do, regardless of the outcome. He is the bread of life, the biscuit. The warm response of others—again, that is just gravy.

Our research findings with adults who are involved in community service affirm this understanding of the role of service in the lives of Christians. In our research, we found that, when compared with other Christians sitting beside them in church on Sunday who are not involved in community service, those serving others through community ministry engage significantly more in the practices of Christian faith. They have the deepest prayer lives and spend more time studying the Scriptures and talking with one another about what it means to be Christian in this world.[5] The commandments to love God and love neighbor are not two different routes to eternal life; they are bound together in Jesus' teaching and in the lives of these Christians. Jesus identifies this love as the way to eternal life, a life not rooted in this world but in the eternity of the God who made heaven and earth.

TABLE 1

Christian Faith Practices of Those Involved in Community Ministry
Compared to Those Not Involved

[1 = never, 2 = rarely, 3 = once in a while, 4 = sometimes,
5 = often, 6 = almost always, 7 = always]

	All respondents n = 7,403	Community ministry participants n = 3,443	Community ministry nonparticipants n = 3,554
I attend weekly worship services.	6.19	6.43	5.96
I pray.	6.14	6.28	5.99
I give financial support to my church.	5.88	6.13	5.62
I practice being tolerant of others' failures by encouraging them.	5.66	5.83	5.49
I forgive and work toward healing relationships with others.	5.34	5.51	5.16
I confess my faults to others.	4.63	4.82	4.43
I discuss Christian responses to contemporary issues with other Christians.	4.34	4.83	3.86
I participate in Bible study activity.	4.33	4.93	3.74
I provide hospitality and care to strangers.	4.05	4.46	3.63
I share the Christian story with others (evangelism).	3.98	4.39	3.56
I volunteer time to help those less fortunate.	3.96	4.73	3.22
I study the history of the Christian church (creeds, confessions, catechism).	3.90	4.28	3.49
I participate in activities that promote social justice in society.	3.27	3.87	2.66
Overall mean	**4.74**	**5.12**	**4.36**

TABLE 2

Length of Community Ministry Involvement and Practices of Faith

Mean scores for . . .

Practices of faith	0–5 years* (n = 303)	6–11** years (n = 278)	12 years or more (n = 271)
I share the Christian story with others (evangelism).	4.00	4.32	4.33
I give financial support to my church.	6.24	6.44	6.61
I provide hospitality and care to strangers.	4.07	4.49	4.72
I volunteer time to help those less fortunate.	4.64	5.04	5.13
I participate in activities that promote social justice in society.	3.32	4.06	4.30
I discuss Christian responses to contemporary issues with other Christians.	4.49	4.91	5.13
Overall Mean	**4.92**	**5.16**	**5.29**

All of the scores in the 0–5 year category are significantly lower (p ≤ .01) than those in the other two categories.
**No significant difference in scores between the 6–11 year category and the 12+ year category.*

The Relationship between Christian Love of Neighbor and Social Work

Because I am dean of a social work school in a Christian university, well-meaning folks often tell me about their own or others' "social work" with persons in poverty or children at risk of failure at school. What they mean is that they are trying to make a significant difference for good in the lives of those they serve as volunteers. Indeed, Christian neighborly care and social work are related, but they are also different. That difference is more than the fact that one gets a paycheck for the services and the other does not.

The relationship of social work and Christian ministry begins in a rich shared history. The profession of social work was birthed by the church; the first social workers were actually volunteers who were deeply concerned about the horrific poverty and misery in the cities that resulted from the Industrial Revolution of the late nineteenth and early twentieth centuries. Jane Addams, one of the most famous of the early social workers, founded Hull House in Chicago in 1889, "a settlement house" that was a combination home and community center; here, middle-class women lived in the slums to provide educational programs, kindergartens for children of working mothers, cultural events, and community organizing to tackle the social problems that grew with industrialization and urbanization. Addams was actively involved in her church and saw Hull House as a living out of her faith and the faith of the others who lived and served with her.[6] More than forty years later, Peter Maurin and Dorothy Day founded the Catholic Worker movement. Much like settlement houses, Catholic Worker houses were resident communities where volunteers as well as members of religious orders shared housing, food, material resources, and companionship with the poor and worked together to serve social problems.[7] Some church volunteers formed organizations that linked volunteers with persons in poverty to provide encouragement as they tried to improve their condition. Still others founded orphanages and foster programs to provide for children whose parents were too impoverished to care for them.

Jane Addams had close ties to the Chicago Training School, founded by the deaconess movement of the Methodist tradition. "Training schools," established by a number of Christian denominations at the turn of the twentieth century, were actually the first schools of social work. These schools were organized by women who wanted to express their Christian faith through service but were not allowed to receive ministry education in male-only church institutions.[8] In these schools, women received the education they needed to become missionaries. Graduates established and managed settlement houses, hospitals, schools, and orphanages for the poor in the United States and throughout the world.[9]

Early on, then, social work and Christian volunteering were virtually the same. As the new vocation, "social work," developed, young professionals began to distinguish themselves from the volunteers. The social work profession attempted to apply the findings of the new social sciences to the societal problems of the day. "Neighboring" was no longer the focus; the focus became applying the new knowledge of the social sciences to the intractable social problems created by the rise of industrial cities. As the social work profession developed, professionals increasingly defined themselves as distinct from well-meaning volunteers motivated by faith. By the last half of the twentieth Century, social work schools were communicating that Christian faith had no place in professional social work—even though many social workers were still motivated by their faith to seek professional education.[10] Despite the distancing of the social work profession from the church, there is still much overlap: social workers are certainly often motivated by faith, and volunteers certainly want to bring about significant change (see figure 2 on p. 99).

Over the past thirty years, state and federal governments have provided fewer and fewer human services, and so there have been fewer professional social workers working with the social problems in our communities, and with those vulnerable populations groups living on the economic and social margins. At the same time, government officials have challenged congregations to take up the slack providing mentoring for families going from welfare to work or intensive job and life skills classes for unemployed and underemployed folks.[11] Much of this work has been carried on by church volunteers, just like the first social workers a century ago. Some government leaders have called for professional social services to be replaced by the services of faith-motivated volunteers. Instead of a social worker, would it not be better to provide the "free" services of a committed volunteer? In a speech to religious leaders in Philadelphia in 2002, President Bush said, "No government policy can put hope in people's hearts or a sense of purpose in people's lives. That is done when someone, some good soul puts an arm around a neighbor and says, 'God loves you, and I love you, and you can count on us both.'"[12] Indeed, everyone needs someone to give that kind of support during troubling times.

Loving volunteers cannot replace the need for social work, however. Social work is a profession, like medicine is a profession. A loving adult (parent or grandparent or friend) who picks up a crying child who has fallen off a bicycle and scraped the skin from both knees may effectively pick out the gravel embedded in the scrapes, apply an antibiotic, and put on bandages while talking tenderly and soothingly. The adult may hold the child in a warm hug, rocking and soothing, until the stinging stops and calm is restored. If it seems a bone is broken or stitches are needed, the adult will give first aid and soothe—and then carry the child to an emergency room. Certainly, the adult has provided medical care, but that does not mean the adult is a physician or a nurse. A physician can set and cast a bone or put in stitches; most loving adults cannot (and do not want to!). But at the same time, the loving adult can provide the rocking and soothing and carrying and reassurance that will probably not be provided by the doctor, no matter how loving and caring the doctor is. The loving and soothing and rocking are not the job of the doctor; that is a loving adult's responsibility and privilege. A seriously hurt child needs both a loving adult and a medical professional. It is not either/or but both/and. We want doctors primarily to focus on setting the bone or putting in stitches; we would not be happy with a doctor who merely comforts without setting or stitching. In the same way, we would never want a parent to try to set a bone or put in stitches—unless they are shipwrecked with no medical care available.

Social workers are like the physician; Christian volunteers are like the loving adult. Both provide care, but the nature of their care has a different focus. A critical need of persons in crisis or facing life challenges is for a strong, compassionate support system, and that is exactly the need that Christians can address with their care. A mother whose child has died, an immigrant who does not speak English, a caregiver of a beloved spouse who is rapidly declining with Alzheimer's disease, a teenager who is faced with the dangers of the streets and the promised protection of a street gang—all of these need the compassionate care and presence that Christian friends, volunteers, can provide. All of us need people who will listen to our struggles, who will be there for us, who will help out in a pinch and love us no matter what happens. Sometimes that coming-alongside friendship is just what is needed to encourage someone to turn their life around.

Often, however, another resource is needed in addition to a befriending presence. Bones are broken; gaping wounds need stitches. That mother whose child has died needs the presence and love of friends, but she may also need professional counseling to help with grief and depression that overwhelms her and threatens her ability to work or care for other children. The immigrant certainly can use a volunteer tutor in English, but he can also use a professional who can help him navigate the complexities of obtaining legal status, finding employment, and maneuvering other social systems in a strange culture. The caregiver needs friends who can give respite from the constancy of responsibilities. But she may also need a professional to help determine the level of care that the beloved spouse with Alzheimer's disease needs, to make the very difficult decision of when home is no longer a safe place, and to locate a support group of other caregivers. The teenager needs not only a friend who believes in and encourages him to stay in school and out of the gangs, but also a social worker who can help organize the community to eradicate gang activity in the school and neighborhood, to provide safe places in school and out of school for students who want to succeed but are afraid, to empower parents to work together for the sake of their children. Finally, those Christian volunteers who are offering friendship, support, and mentoring may well need a social worker to help them develop the knowledge and skills to offer friendship and support rugged enough to withstand the crises they are helping others to face.[13]

The flaw in the thinking that volunteers might be able to do better what professional social workers can do is either/or thinking. Persons and communities in crisis do not need either volunteers or professionals—they need both! They need *both* compassionate Christians who will pour themselves out in service *and* social workers— who may also be compassionate Christians. Many social workers have chosen to be professionals so that they can bring professional knowledge and skills to bear on the most difficult problems facing families and communities in our world.

The difference between compassionate servant-volunteers and compassionate social workers is not whether or not they are motivated by their faith. The difference is the goal of their work with the one being served. For the servant-volunteer, the *primary* goal is presence and compassion. We serve because we care and because we serve a God who cares. No mother should have to grieve alone, so we come to grieve with her. No child should face the streets alone, so we come to be friend and encourager. Of course, servant-volunteers also bring their life experiences and connections and resources, and those resources may be vital catalysts for major changes in the lives of those they serve. Those resources should always be offered in the context of presence and compassion.

For the social worker, the *primary* goal is change—setting bones, stitching wounds—and then perhaps assessing the need for bike paths to prevent bike accidents. The social worker forms a contract with those served to do some specified work with a hoped-for outcome. The mother must learn how to manage her grief and go on with her life for the sake of those who depend on her, and for her own sake. The teenager wants to stay in school and out of the gangs, and social workers can help the teenager, the teenager's family and school, and the larger community to make ways for that to happen. Ultimately, social workers' service is measured by how effective they are in being a catalyst for the change that they and those they serve agree is the goal of their work together. That service ideally is offered within a context of presence and compassion, but presence and compassion are not the primary focus of a professional relationship.

In sum, servant-volunteers' service is measured by how faithfully they have served and by the extent to which they have been compassionate, even if the one they have served has not changed at all. Certainly, social workers need and want those served to experience them as faithful and compassionate, and servant-volunteers want to be catalysts for hoped-for change. Their work overlaps, but the emphasis is different. Social workers focus on the task they agree to undertake

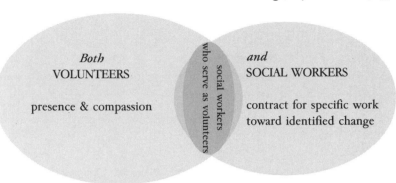

Figure 1—The relationship between Christian care of volunteers and professional social work

with those served. Servant-volunteers focus on the relationship they offer, the kindness that they seek to embody.

Christian families have dinners with tablecloths and good dishes on a Thursday night and sit down with people who are homeless for a meal. They go every week—every week—delivering meals to the homebound. They tutor children and mentor teenagers who might otherwise fail in school. They teach computer literacy and workplace skills to young single mothers so they can find decent jobs. Their motivation comes not because a government official says, "The poor folks are your responsibility." Their motivation comes from a God who calls them to live their faith by caring for a neighbor.

Thy Kingdom Come

Jesus taught us to pray, "Your kingdom come, your will be done, on earth as it is in heaven" (Matt 6:10). Our prayer is not passively waiting for God to deliver the kingdom; Jesus went on to teach us to go after it, to "strive first for the kingdom of God, and his righteousness" (Matt 6:33). We serve as Christians because we love God, and we yearn for God's ways to be our ways. We yearn for Jubilee, for justice, for God's kingdom on earth as it is in heaven. Our yearning stirs us to seek the kingdom here, in this life, in our lives. We seek by living in our lives what the kingdom of God looks like.

We look for the kingdom with our actions more than our eyes. Like blind persons, we cannot always see it, so we reach for it, we feel for it. We feel for it by serving those who need our care. We also seek justice by tackling the social structures that lead to poverty and violence and discouragement in the lives of God's children. Doing so communicates to others that God is committed to seeing justice acted out by his people.[14] Such small projects are actually *seeds* out of which will come God's kingdom.[15] With our hands, we push the seeds into the soil of our communities. Our service plants the germinating seeds of the reign of God on Earth; we cannot see the seeds swelling and bursting forth. We sometimes glimpse the first shoots pushing up, but they seem so small. Building houses for poor people will not eliminate all the slums. It is a start, however, and we pray that God will receive our work and miraculously expand it, like the loaves and fishes, into the fulfillment of God's will for the world.

It is not that our work, however dedicated and skillful and faith-filled, can make the kingdom come. It is not our efforts that control the in-breaking of God's kingdom. Some of those first church volunteers who responded to the desperate poverty created by the Industrial Revolution were convinced that if Christians would just seek hard enough, they could improve the world over time and by their own efforts, usher in God's kingdom. The outbreak of World War I dashed their hopes. The kingdom is God's, not ours, to bring. We pray for it; we feel for it by acting in ways that give a glimpse of what the jubilation will be like—and we also wait.

In our seeking of the kingdom, we recognize, too, that mercy must be paired with justice. Children need broken bones repaired— and bike paths to provide safe places to ride. Both building houses for poor people (service) and eradicating poverty (justice) are important. Love kindness *and* seek justice—in the context of keeping in step with God. The next step for the Samaritan would have been seeking justice for travelers. It is not enough to pick up naked, bleeding neighbors and check them into a motel where they can heal. Justice would mean working to clean up the crime along that road with safety patrols, street lights, and maybe some gang intervention to steer would-be robbers to a better way of making a living.

Our faith in God and the kingdom to come is about *doing;* "faith by itself, if it has no works, is dead" (Jas 2:17). Faithful action flows from belief about what is real and what is important. Jesus taught us to be active, storing up treasures for ourselves in heaven, not on Earth, where moth and rust destroy. "For where your treasure is, there your heart will be also" (Matt 6:21). We treasure that which we think has value. That treasure is what we give our hearts to, what we trust. In other words, our service not only grows out of our faith, but service also turns around and shapes our faith. Sometimes our experiences in serving others confirm our beliefs, and sometimes they pull those beliefs into question.

Heather and Jim Hall believed that God calls us to love our neighbors as ourselves, and so they led their family to meet and play with and learn to love the neighborhood children in the summer recreation program. Their beliefs led them to trust that God was with them in this service experience—and they acted. They put everybody in the car on Tuesday evenings and went to serve across town. Their service led to several outcomes: new relationships, a new understanding of the challenges these children faced in growing up in a drug- and gang-infested community, a new appreciation that mere presence is a powerful gift we give to one another. Those experiences—outcomes— led them to a deeper understanding of God's compassion, of what it means to trust in a God who took on human form to serve and to love us in the midst of all the challenges of our lives.

Sometimes serving deepens and confirms our faith because we get a glimpse that God is working through us in the lives of others. Perhaps one of the children's parents will tell the Halls that, because they are providing care one night a week for her children, she has been able to take a course in community college and is thinking about working toward a college degree. Or perhaps a child on the playground says, "I want to know more about the Jesus you read to us about in that story." The Halls can rejoice that God is using them to plant kingdom seeds. They are "donkeys" with a great bit part in the good news drama.

The Connection of Service to Faith

The outcomes are not always what we expect or wish for, however. The impact of service on our faith does not just depend on what happens, but how we come to understand what happens. What if Heather and Jim's daughter, Sarah, is shot by a stray bullet in a drive-by shooting while they are at the church playground? They will most certainly be devastated and horrified that their decision placed their child in harm's way. But how will they understand it? Will they question the existence of a God who allows defenseless children who are just trying to live into what it means to "love neighbor" to be hurt in such a seemingly senseless way? Or will they develop a deeper sense of compassion for parents whose children spend all of their days at risk of gunshot wounds? Will they believe that God caused the gunshot and so hold God responsible? Or will they believe that God agonizes with them? Or will they try to hold both of the beliefs simultaneously? Will they make the connection that God sent his own child into service, only to see him murdered by those he went to serve? Will they no longer trust in a God who allows such things to happen? Or will they develop a deeper trust in a God who wants justice and kindness and protection for all children, not just their own middle-class children? Will they become even more deeply involved in the community, not just in the recreation program, but also in seeking ways to rid the community of gangs and violence?

We believe, we trust those beliefs as truth that leads us to action—in this case, to service. The service has consequences for us and for those we serve. We think about, reflect on, try to make sense out of those consequences, given what we believed when we started. And those reflections in turn alter, refine, deepen, or even destroy those beliefs. Faith is thus a cycle. Faith leads to trust and then to action. Those actions have outcomes, or consequences. And as we reflect on those outcomes, the beliefs from which our actions derive are altered or deepened.

Thus far, we have focused on the actions (and their outcomes) that flow from our beliefs and are the outward evidence of our faith. That service has to be connected to our beliefs and our relationship

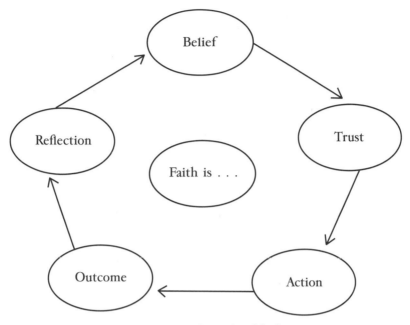

Figure 2—The cycle of faith

with God. Our conversation with God in prayer, our worship in a community of faith, our study and reflection on the Bible and the history of the church and the life experiences of other fellow journeyers are part of this dance between reflection and action that make up the life of faith.

For two thousand years, some Christians in every generation have decided to live their faith by leaving families for a solitary life, where they can devote themselves to meditation and prayer. Some came to believe that an ascetic life of prayer and study was holier than a life of action and service, much like the division that seemed to develop between the deacons in the early church who were engaged in service and the church leaders who focused on study and prayer and preaching. As we saw in the life of Stephen, it is a false division.

Family life and service in the community are significant contexts in which we live our faith. But just as going away indefinitely to pray and study alone seems lopsided, so is a life of service that does not include the "inner" disciplines of Christian faith—those that focus on what we know and believe. We need to reflect on our experiences in light of that knowledge and those beliefs. Just as service is faith in action for families, there are also ways that we need to engage in reflection on our faith as families. There is an extensive literature on what are called the "spiritual disciplines."[16] I want to focus on six disciplines that appear to be most important to the understanding and reflecting on our faith together as families. They are:

- Worshipping God together.

- Telling and reading the Christian story to one another, from the Bible and as God has continued to work in the world through history.

- Living our faith in our relationships with one another.

- Praying—listening and talking with God—together.

- Giving our money, time, and other resources for the work of the church and to care for the needs of others.

- Welcoming others into our homes and to our tables.

These faith practices are not just more activities to be slotted onto the family calendar, however. Instead, they can be woven throughout our time together and apart. Prayer can be done "on schedule" over meals or at other times, but it can also be breathed as we slog through the day, as we drive together to or from the places we serve or work or go to school. One of the challenges for us is that many adult Christians did not grow up with these practices, so they do not come naturally. If we did not learn them as children, however, we can learn them as adults.[17]

Worshipping God

Worship includes giving thanks to God, singing and speaking words of praise, and receiving the sacraments given to us in Christ. We most often think of worship as the planned experience we have together with others in our congregation on Sunday morning and other times in the week and year. Going together as a family to worship God with the larger community of faith shapes our understanding and beliefs and experience of God in ways we cannot put into words. Worship with other Christians expresses our faith and feeds our faith. Jesus told his disciples to share the bread and the wine together as an act of worship, done in remembrance of him and pointing to his coming again (Luke 22:18-20). Similarly, singing to one another and to God together is worship (Eph 5:19). In addition to gathering with the congregation, families can remember the Lord over the supper table and sing praises together as they do chores or drive down the highway together.

In my study of faith in family life, I found that those families who eat regular meals together have richer stories of faith than those who do not. Worship can be high and holy at church, but it can also be low and holy over macaroni and cheese when we share it together at home, remembering the God who gives us all we have. Worship can also be shared as we squish our bare toes in ocean sand or backyard grass or a pebbly creek and sing praise or say prayers to the God who created us for one another and everything in this amazing world. Worship reminds us that in our service to others, we are donkeys in the Palm Sunday parade.

Telling and Reading the Christian Story to One Another

The Christian story includes, of course, the Bible, as well as the story of how God has worked in the world for the past two thousand years and is working even now. Making Bible reading a part of daily life together is a discipline that takes practice. Like physical exercise, it is important to start with something simple enough that your family can do it and feel like you have accomplished something. When you let other activities crowd it out of your daily life, start over. Reflect together on how biblical teachings help you understand the experience of service.

Living Our Faith in Our Relationships with One Another

The simple and very difficult challenge of loving our families is also a Christian practice—and it takes practice! Jesus taught that our relationships with one another are to reflect God's love (1 John 4:16-21). All through the Scriptures, God's love is portrayed in family relationships. That love is a rugged, active love that endures hard times, not the romantic falling-in-love feelings that come and go. Family members disappoint and even hurt one another deeply. The prophet Hosea loved Gomer, his wife who kept running off into prostitution. He kept taking her back and used his troubled family to illustrate God's love for the people of God, however unfaithful. In the parable of the prodigal son, the father took the wayward son back and also loved the grumpy elder brother, looking for him, too, and inviting him to the party. So God folds us into parental arms of love. The endurance of family love points to the endurance of God's love: "love never ends" (1 Cor 13:8).

Although love certainly involves sacrifice of self, even to the point of giving one's life, such self-giving is not the ultimate aim but rather a means to the end of mutual love. Even Jesus' ultimate sacrifice of his life for unrepentant sinners was aimed at restoring us to relationship with God, to mutual love. Parents love infants who cannot yet focus their eyes or recognize them, much less reciprocate that love. Over time, however, there is the expectation that children will learn to love their parents in return. And parents dream and hope that their children, drawing lines to divide the territory of the car backseat as eight- and ten-year-olds, will grow up to want to spend Thanksgiving together, to be friends as well as siblings, to come from being scattered across the country to play football together with grandsons and nephews in the empty field next to the house.

God's grace sustains us as we stumble through life together, making mistakes, losing our tempers, becoming weary and sloppy in our relationships with one another. We have the opportunity to live as Jesus taught us in the day-in and day-out of family life, as we confess and tell the truth to one another, repent, forgive one another, share our burdens and joys with one another. Family life gives us a great training ground for all these characteristics of the Christian life. We experience grace from one another. Families teach us that God truly does work a process of miracles in our lives. We learn through the experiences of family life the truth of Jesus' promise that those who sacrifice their lives will truly find life.

Praying—Listening and Talking with God—Together

Prayer together can take many forms. It can be as simple as, "Go with us, God. Help us know what to do," in the car, wide-eyed as you drive together to where you are going to serve. Or similarly on the way home, "Thank you, God, for being with us today. We don't know how to help sometimes, but we know you do." Families can pray together for those they serve and for one another. Some families find that saying memorized prayers together at mealtimes, bedtimes, and other times keeps them rooted in their faith together. Spontaneous prayers of thanksgiving for sunsets, the sound of the rain on the roof, the warmth of the furnace on a cold night, keep us remembering where all good gifts come from. Our families are branches of the vine, not trees standing alone (John 15:1-3); prayer is the connection to the vine.

Giving Our Money, Time, and Other Resources for the Work of the Church and to Care for the Needs of Others

This whole book has been about giving of our time, but families have other resources. Brad and Lisa, whom you met in chapter 1, talked about how they share their financial resources with those in need. Sometimes it is easiest for the family member who pays the bills to simply make out the checks for church offerings, for gifts to charity and needs around the world. Talking about the choices being made, however, allows everyone in the family to participate in the decision to share the family's resources.

Welcoming Others into Our Homes and to Our Tables

It often feels much easier to peel a check out of the checkbook than it is to open our lives and our family home to others, particularly the "stranger." Christian hospitality is quite different from what our society thinks of: cleaning house and taking the protective towels off the arms of chairs because "company" is coming, preparing a special meal for friends, using the good dishes in the dining room instead of eating in the kitchen. Christian hospitality is not synonymous with "entertaining." Entertaining refers to a break in a family's routine in order to take care of visitors in special ways, different from ordinary daily life. It means putting on our best behavior, being fancier than our everyday ways.

In contrast, true hospitality means inviting people—strangers—into the heart of the family as a valued representative of Christ's presence. That can be symbolized by pizza over the kitchen table or other ways we truly make others feel "at home." It is welcoming children's friends to spend the night, newcomers in the neighborhood to a simple meal in our kitchen on their moving day, neighbor children into our living room to do their homework until a parent can come home from work. Christine Pohl points out that hospitality in the early church and for many centuries thereafter meant offering to strangers the food, shelter, and protection of our homes.[18] The writer of Hebrews urged readers not to "neglect to show hospitality to strangers, for by doing that some have entertained angels without knowing it" (Heb 13:2).

Hospitality is very hard because it makes us vulnerable. The neighbor child who comes over today may also show up tomorrow, and the day after, and the day after. The new neighbors invited to supper may stay too long and interfere with what we really need to do. The troubled youngster we take in as a foster child might actually steal from us or in other ways abuse the privilege of being folded into the family. At the least, hospitality is often inconvenient.

The need often overwhelms our hospitality. Where do we draw the line? Christine Pohl describes being a member of a small church that welcomed and resettled hundreds of refugees as an expression of the biblical teachings about hospitality and welcoming strangers. It was an enormous job. Some of those they took in were grateful; some were not. Some actually became friends and joined the congregation. The congregation experienced firsthand the biblical stories of the blessings from strangers to whom hospitality was extended. The widow fed a stranger her last bit of bread, only to be blessed by unfailing provisions and the restoration of life in her son (1 Kgs 17:8-24). The prostitute Rahab welcomed the spies into her house and gained protection for her whole family (Josh 2:1-21). The woman at the well gave a strange rabbi a drink from her own dipper and received in return "living water" (John 4:7-30).

Ultimately, hospitality transforms the other into an insider, not an outsider. Those children from the neighborhood became the grandchildren Susan and Mark would otherwise never have had. Strangers sometimes become friends. The goal of all Christian hospitality is to be transformed into the fellowship of the kingdom of God, where the distinction between insiders and outsiders, between those who belong and those who do not, is broken down. Hospitality thus points us to the kingdom of God.

A Seamless Garment

Our faith is meant to be a seamless garment of belief and trust in God, service to neighbors, prayer for them and for ourselves, worship, giving, hospitality, and encouraging and loving one another. We pray as we serve. Our service sends us scrambling to our knees asking for guidance and to the Bible to remember why we are doing what we are doing. Our service tires us and challenges us and gives us ample opportunity to encourage one another and forgive one another and love on one another.

Moreover, our families are embedded in a larger community of faith, the congregation. Congregations should be vital resources for families living their faith together in service and in worship. The final chapter explores what we have learned about the ways congregations support and strengthen families for service.

Christian social workers may serve as professionals who are motivated by their faith, but as professionals, they are primarily contracting for specific work with clients and are not primarily there to serve as compassionate friends. If they are serving as volunteers, in the overlapping area, then they need to be clear about their role, either as volunteer or as professional.

6

Becoming an Inside Out Congregation

Service needs to be at the very heart of Christian education and the life of a congregation. It is a significant factor in growing the faith of Christians because it is a central theme in Jesus' teaching. Not all Christian service and work for justice needs to be part of congregational life, but certainly, every congregation needs to place service and work for justice at the heart of life together. The Christians we interviewed engage in service individually and with their families. Some are part of service and justice activities sponsored by their congregations. Others found their places of service with little involvement by or even knowledge on the part of their congregational leaders. This chapter explores what the congregations we studied taught us about developing a congregational culture of service.

It is the role of leaders to help congregants develop a taste for ministry. Like a wine-tasting party, consider having service-tasting parties, so that everyone has an opportunity for a taste. Some congregations are deciding to close the doors with a "Gone Serving" sign out, and turn the congregation out into the community in a blitz of service projects. The opportunities are limited only by your imagination—cleaning a park, mowing lawns of frail elderly neighbors, painting fire hydrants, holding a neighborhood movie night by showing old movies on the side of the church and popping popcorn, inviting the neighborhood to a cookout for Sunday lunch, washing cars for free, going door to door in the church's neighborhood with a small gift from the church just to say, "We want to be your neighbor." The goal is not to spend a day and be done with service, but rather to spend a day as a taste. Not all, but some families will be hooked and be ready to make a commitment to be involved for more than a day.

Developing an Inside Out Culture

We chose congregations to study that had gone beyond service tasting to become what we came to call "inside out congregations." In an inside out congregation, everyone has opportunity and is encouraged to be engaged in service outside the congregation, in the community. Everyone! Rusaw and Swanson say that the minimum qualification for serving should be breathing.[1] Babies can minister when they go in the arms of a parent or grandparent to visit a homebound neighbor. Senior adults who are confined to their homes can develop a phone friendship with a child in an afterschool church program. The child can provide a friendship in return. Everyone can do something. There is no poverty deeper than having nothing to give; service provides opportunity for everyone to have a meaningful "rich" life with others.

How do congregations find their way into the service engagement that becomes their signature in the community? Many congregations are inundated with requests from organizations needing volunteers and financial support. Of all the agencies that need volunteers, schools that need tutors, nursing homes that need visitors, literacy courses that need teachers, job-skills workshops that need leaders, and social policies that need to be advocated, how does a congregation find its own calling? As part of the Service and Faith project, we studied the in-depth interviews we conducted in congregations with inside out cultures. We interviewed twenty-nine congregational leaders, twenty-five actively engaged congregational members, and an additional sixteen families engaged together in service. From these interviews, we learned the following seven basic steps for congregations to get involved, stay involved, and nurture an inside out culture.[2]

A "Catalyst" Proposes That the Congregation Become Involved

Congregations often have members who are professionals in the community—teachers, police officers, social workers. Congregational members also serve on community boards or volunteer in other ways. The congregations we studied saw these members who are already active in the community as ready-made linkages to service opportunities. As one pastor said, "We say to the social service professionals in our congregations, 'Teach us; help us; show us; walk with us; bring those people to us.'" Pastors and other congregation leaders also serve on community boards and as advisors to government officials, developing relationships that lead to service partnerships.

These community professionals and leaders—whether congregational members or staff persons—served as "catalysts." You may remember from high school chemistry class that a catalyst is an agent that precipitates a reaction between two other agents that otherwise do not interact with one another. The "catalyst" for congregation involvement is someone who has one foot in the congregation and the other ankle deep in the needs of the larger community. They serve as a human connector of congregation with community and can speak in the congregation with authority based in their firsthand community experience.[3] In contrast, none of the congregations we studied had become involved because someone from the *outside*, who had no role in the congregation, asked them. Government officials and social service agencies may approach congregations as resources for community service, but there has to be a link with someone inside the congregation already connected and willing to act. One pastor served as the ride-along chaplain with the sheriff's department and saw community needs firsthand. He was able to use that knowledge in helping his church target ministry needs. Staff members in another church saw a man begging for food on the sidewalk outside their church as they were leaving to have lunch together. They invited the man to walk with them and join them for a meal at a nearby café. That experience led eventually to a feeding program for the homeless, located in the church's fellowship hall, and then a counseling program to link them with the services they needed to find and keep permanent homes.

Practice principle: Identify the catalysts in your congregation. Learn about their connections in the community. Ask them about possible roles of your congregation in community service and community action.

The Congregation Determines if the Ministry Fits Their Identity as a Community

Every congregation has a process for deciding what the congregation will do—what kind of carpet to put in the foyer, whether or not to have a Christmas concert, how to spend the congregation's financial resources. There may be a formal group, or an informal group, or simply one or a few individuals who consider and decide such matters. Such a vetting process is required before the congregation will embrace a service initiative as its own.

Part of that vetting needs to be assessing the nature of volunteer relationships that will be encouraged. The most engaging ministry opportunities for congregations are those that have opportunities for volunteers to develop relationships both with recipients and also with one another. Congregations identify themselves as faith *communities*, and so the building and strengthening of relationships is an important function of all congregational activity, including community service. For example, a Lutheran pastor said to us, "All our ministries need to contribute to community building."

Ideally, service opportunities need to allow cross-generational family involvement, so that whole families can serve, from the youngest to the oldest. Some must participate in the service project alone, either because they live alone or their families do not choose to join them or participate in the life of the congregation. The service project then becomes a wonderful opportunity for leaders to link them with others in the congregation. Jesus sent out his disciples in pairs (Luke 10:1; see Acts 13:2; 15:27, 39-40; 17:14; 19:22); no one should serve alone. Serving together adds both companionship and accountability. Instead of deacons splitting up to visit the homebound, two deacons can take with them two of the teenagers from the youth group. Everyone benefits. The teenagers are treated like full-fledged, participating members of the congregation who have an important role to play in ministry. They have opportunity to know both the deacons and those they visit, people with lives and stories. Such a service provides a far more meaningful experience for teenagers than participating in the youth choir singing in nursing home hallways to anonymous persons in wheelchairs. In a visit to specific older adults, those visited may be delighted to meet and form relationships with teenagers. Ideally, the service team will wrap the service in conversation together, perhaps over a hamburger afterward. They learn from one another—deacons something about the young people in the midst of their congregation, and teens about the ministry of visiting and the meaning of such ministry in the life of faith. The adults on the ministry team have opportunity to form friendships with teenagers, potentially addressing the adult deprivation most teenagers suffer from today.[4] If this relationship continues over time, the deacons are serving in the role of "faith-grandparents" and the teenagers as "faith-grandchildren." With just a little prodding from a church leader who serves as a different kind of matchmaker, faith-families grow organically in the rich soil of service together.[5]

Not all service opportunities lend themselves to cross-generational involvement, but even when that is not possible, everyone in service through the congregation should be part of a team. Bill Hybels describes how even folks mowing the church lawn need to be part of a team, not simply showing up and working alone and going home, but rather beginning the work session with a time spent together as a mowing team, a time when they can laugh, share, and pray together, accompanied by donuts and coffee.[6] Often, service teams become friendships that extend beyond the service project.

When there was not initially the opportunity for cross-generational involvement, the congregations we studied often figured out a way to change the ministry itself. For example, a Presbyterian congregation had created cross-generational activities to accompany the building of affordable housing in their community. Because of safety concerns, children were not allowed at the home-building sites while construction was taking place. Meanwhile, back at the church, children and adults together made doorstops, planters, and birdhouses to give as gifts to the new homeowners.

In Genesis 33, Jacob meets Esau many years after he had cheated him out of their father's blessing, which was supposed to have gone to Esau as the firstborn. Jacob is not at all sure how his brother might receive him. Graciously, Esau suggests that they travel together. Jacob responds that he must travel slowly, because his flocks and herds are nursing lambs and calves, and he also had many small children. Jacob says that he will travel at the pace of the children. That is a good pace for the church. Our life and our service must include even the littlest among us.

Practice principle: In considering whether or not to adopt a service project or program, determine if it can be engaged in by cross-generational family groups or teams. If not, are there ways it can be modified to include cross-generational service or, if that is not possible, team involvement? Adopt or adapt service projects and programs that fit the family and community life of the congregation.

The Congregation Evaluates Their Capacity

At the same time they are looking at the "fit" of a ministry with their identity as a congregation, congregation leaders are also eyeing what the ministry will demand of them and whether they have the capacity to sustain the ministry. Capacity involves having the people resources (i.e., volunteers, leadership), facilities, funding, and necessary community connections.

Assessment of the people resources could be as simple as phoning potential families for the proposed ministry to see who might be interested. Several leaders said that one purpose of this assessment was to avoid competition between ministries. A pastor explained that they had a tutoring ministry that was very exciting and they had more than forty-two adults engaged in the nearby elementary school, but then they could not find enough teachers for their Sunday school because the most likely teachers had chosen instead to become tutors. Another pastor talked about the importance of staying focused. He sees his role as holding that focus and not allowing the congregation to be swamped by trying to respond to multiple and competing needs in the community.

We also learned that if a congregation did not have the resources that it needed to launch a service or justice project, that assessment did not preclude the congregation's involvement. If the activity seemed important and the congregation felt called to do it, then leaders made it a priority in prayer. Together, the congregation prayed that God would provide the resources needed. In other words, the fit with the congregation's sense of identity and calling was more important than whether they had the resources at the ready.

One of the filters used to determine whether the congregation would become involved was the extent to which the project fit the congregation's gifts. Pastors explained that their role is not to start with the needs in the community and find persons to address them, but rather to identify the gifts of the congregation and find ways they can use those gifts in the community. Their model of discipleship, as one pastor said, is to "fan the flames of those gifts." At the same time, Hybels points out that spiritual gifts are less something to be figured out ahead of time and more what God reveals to us as we serve.[7] Callings and gifts tend to evolve over time and in a dance with one another. Sometimes the calling to serve takes the lead and gifts are discovered in the process of serving. Other times, the gifts take the lead and pull the congregation into a particular service arena. In either case, the focus does not begin with identifying all the needs of the community and then trying to figure out how to address them.

Sometimes these congregations had developed partnerships with other community organizations in order to have the resources for a community ministry. Sometimes they collaborated with other congregations so that together there would be enough volunteers. They also recruited professionals from community organizations to train and provide consultation to volunteers. Developing partnerships with others in the community provides multiple ways of serving that congregations could never do on their own and multiple layers of service. Congregation volunteers come alongside community servants—social workers, public school teachers, health providers—helping them as they both help the community.

In addition to the people power, congregations considered how their physical facilities might be used. Many congregations allow community programs to use their facilities at low or no cost, and those programs become identified with the congregation. One church that initially agreed to house an agency's homeless feeding program found that those who came for meals were trying to sponge bathe themselves in the restroom sinks, so instead of banning that use of their facility, they remodeled the bathrooms to add showers and provided towels and lockers for persons who are homeless to store their belongings. Although the ministry started out as an external entity using the church's facility, a good way to use otherwise empty space during the week, the congregation "adopted" the ministry over time and at considerable expense.

Practice principle: Assess the people, facilities, finances, and community connections the service project or program will require. If the congregation has those resources, will they come at the expense of another congregational activity? If so, determine priorities. If the congregation does not currently have the resources, determine if partnerships with other organizations or congregations might fill the gaps, or if the project is so vital to the congregation's sense of calling that there is a commitment to pray and begin anyway, trusting that the resources will come.

The Congregation Decides Whether or Not to Commit to the Service Project/Program

If the ministry does not fit the identity or the capacity of the congregation, then it is not adopted as a formal project/program of the congregation. That does not preclude individual members of the congregation from becoming involved, but they do so out of a personal sense of calling and not in a congregation-supported project or program.

If there is a fit both with the congregation's identity and with its resources, then a process of adoption begins. The actual decision to say, "Yes, we're going to do this," may be a formal decision of a recognized leadership structure at a recognized point in time, or an informal commitment may emerge over time. Most, but not all, of the congregations we studied used a formal decision process—a group of leaders voted, or the church discussed at a church meeting and agreed together to invest themselves. Even so, as congregations respond to changing needs, or their understanding of need, the ministries also evolve and one ministry grows from another. For example, one congregation formally agreed to sponsor a short-term program of feeding lunch to older adults while a community organization revamped its senior citizen center. Some persons who were homeless showed up asking if they could eat, too, and so the congregation expanded the program just a bit to include homeless persons. When the senior citizen center was finished, the older adult lunch program moved to the new facility, but the homeless people they had been feeding had become attached to the congregation and the congregation volunteers to them. It did not seem so hard for the congregation to transition the feeding program to be for anyone who needed it. One day, it was very stormy, and volunteers serving in the feeding program just could not face putting persons who were homeless back out into the hard rain after lunch. The one afternoon then led the congregation to develop a transition shelter for homeless families.

The most important factor in a congregation's decision to engage in a new service or advocacy activity appears to be the pastor's support. Pastors not only support the activity by being involved themselves, at least initially, but also by providing through sermons and teaching the theological rationale for service and justice work to be seen as the heart of Christian discipleship. It is not just the pastor, however; it is important that the congregation also be actively engaged in the decision, particularly if the ministry has significant costs attached to it.

Practice principle: If you want the congregation's sanction for a project or program, then determine what the congregation's decision-making practices are and follow those practices, whether formal or informal; they are usually both. As the ministry changes over time, continue to return to the congregation for sanction and support. If the pastor is not a formal part of the decision-making process, be sure to include the pastor in this process and garner the pastor's active involvement, at least through the decision-making and launch of the program or project.

Begin the Project/Program with the Structures
That Will Sustain It over Time

Once the congregation has said yes to a ministry, then it is time to enroll volunteers to serve. Heather Hall's pastor preached a sermon that was the catalyst for her taking her family to the congregation's missions fair and finding a place to serve together. Talking about service opportunities in meetings and church publications may also channel some members into service—but not many, and usually those who are already active in other ways.

The most common catalyst for a volunteer family to become involved in service for the first time is, "Someone asked us," and that someone is often a church leader, whether a lay leader or a staff leader. A director of Christian education explained that he takes church members out for breakfast and suggests how he can use their gifts that he has observed. The personal touch is critical in moving from passive acknowledgment that "we really should get involved" to active personal engagement. A research study of adolescents involved in community service found that 93 percent of young people who were asked to volunteer by someone close to them did volunteer. In contrast, only 24 percent of those who volunteered were not personally asked.[8]

The leaders and volunteers in the congregations we studied described ten factors that they believe have contributed to sustained involvement over time: direct involvement of the congregational leader; volunteer affirmation; financial support; social networking; volunteer training; sharing stories; reflecting on the relationship of service and faith; congregational prayer; a welcoming culture; and ongoing planning. Each of these factors, in turn, contributes to a congregational culture that supports not only a particular ministry but the congregation's continuing and expanding involvement in the community.

Congregational leader directly involved

It is very important for leaders to be actively involved in the ministry, especially in the beginning, setting an example for the rest of the congregation. "Leader" does not always mean the pastor, however; a leader can be anyone who is looked to for setting vision and direction for the faith community.

Affirmed volunteers

Recognizing the work they are doing in the name of the church can affirm and strengthen the engagement of volunteers. Some pastors ask for permission to use stories about the ministry in sermons, or a church leader blesses what a volunteer is doing in a personal interchange—a casual conversation, a handwritten note, or a phone call. The affirmation may not even be personal. A Baptist bank manager on a home care team for persons with HIV/AIDS described sitting in church on a Sunday when she was discouraged and thinking about quitting because some of the other volunteers were not doing what they needed to do. The pastor preached that Sunday on being a "willing worker." She remembered, "He brought it home by saying that, 'It's not about you, it's about what God wants you to do'; he had my number."

Publicity about the ministry can be important for enlisting new volunteers, and at the same time, it affirms those already engaged. Publicity can be blurbs in the church bulletin or newsletter, requests for support spoken in the worship service announcements, and bulletin boards. It is important to show all kinds of families and teams, so that those not already engaged can see people like themselves in the pictures. Rusaw and Swanson recommend giving volunteer leaders disposable cameras and using the pictures they take, or video footage of the ministry, during a worship service or in church publications.[9] Take care to avoid the faces of service recipients or get their permission to be photographed; for children, permission to use photographs must come from their parents.

Sometimes recognition can backfire and be considered offensive when volunteers do not want the attention. A pastor explained:

> In the corporate world, people give plaques to put on their walls. But we take seriously what Jesus said in the Sermon on the Mount, "When you give alms, don't let your left hand know what your right is doing." We are very nervous about praising people for service, as if the reason they were doing it would be to receive

praise. But then again, we want to give thanks for the spirit that is working within them and that is making a difference in people's lives. So there is this very strange balancing.

Leaders need to know the volunteers well enough to know what kind of recognition will be encouraging and affirming for them. It may be their picture on a bulletin board or the gift of a coffee mug or some other symbol of gratitude, but it may also be a book or church sponsorship to attend a workshop that will encourage them and give them new ideas for their involvement. It may be, "I am so grateful for your service; I am praying for you." Affirmation needs to take place over time, not just in the initial engagement in service.

Financial support

One volunteer described the financial gifts of members as a sign that his congregation was proud of the ministry and, by extension, of him. Budget for the service program is very important not just because some programs cannot run without money, but also because it symbolizes to volunteers the ownership and commitment of the congregation to the ministry. It says to them that they are representatives of the congregation worthy of support. Several volunteers spoke of the overwhelming response that comes when they ask for donations—more food than they can use, more clothing than they can give away, money pressed into their hands even when they have not asked. The coordinator for a cold weather shelter for persons who are homeless told me how an elderly woman wants to help but is just not physically able. Instead, she brings two big boxes of oatmeal each month. Other members of her California congregation strip their orange trees so the shelter can have fresh oranges in the morning. With tears glistening in her eyes and choking her voice, she told me that a single mother in the church had brought her a bag of quarters, nickels, and dimes just the week before. The mother's three daughters had built a lemonade stand and had decided to give all the money they made "to the poor people of the church." This kind of support matters far beyond the sustaining of the service program; it is another affirmation of the volunteers who are serving there.

Social networks

Social networks sustain volunteers. A woman in her eighties who teaches budgeting and job skills to poor families told us that she had worried that when she retired she would lose connection with what is going on in the city. Instead, she has made a whole new set of connections with the many volunteers that regularly serve in the ministry beside her. They look forward to their meeting each week where they plan for the future, share experiences, and over time, have come to share their personal lives and struggles with one another. This group of volunteers have really become a community for one another as their commitment to one another has grown through serving together. Families networked with other families engaged together in service have opportunities to share struggles and support one another when their family lives are taking on aspects unusual in the circles of families with whom they may normally associate.

In addition to the social networks of the volunteers themselves, congregations provided networks of other resources that supported the ministry, and therefore, the volunteers. For example, a job-training program in one congregation networked with potential employers in the congregation to locate jobs for graduates. The congregation becomes more anchored to its larger community as it weaves networks of support for the service programs it sponsors and supports. In return, the agencies and other congregations in the network see the congregation as a vital part of the community that they can turn to as well. Just as the social networks among volunteers provide support for their ongoing involvement, the social networks among organizations and congregations sustain and strengthen their work together.

Trained volunteers

Some congregations provide the training of volunteers themselves; others partner with an agency in the community to provide training. Training most often focuses on the culture of the community where the service will be provided more than training in specific skills for the service in which volunteers are engaging. A few congregations offered ministry-specific training, however, such as how to teach English as a second language, provide financial counseling, or tutor first graders in reading. The best training is not simply a one-time workshop but ongoing support from professional leaders who can provide emotional and task support to volunteers in the sometimes challenging work they have undertaken.

Shared stories

Rabbi Nathan of Nemirov, an eighteenth-century Hasidic rabbi, explained that the reason the Torah begins with the stories and not laws is because stories have the power to awaken a person's heart.[10] Some congregations provided opportunities for volunteers or even the service recipients to tell stories of their service in a public gathering, sharing what they were doing and what it meant to them. Such presentations can be wonderful ways to motivate others to find their place to serve. A journalist who taught budgeting skills in a homeless shelter chuckled as he said about his congregation, "They are pleased with me," because he was given opportunities to talk about the ministry. Notice that the congregation was not just pleased that the ministry was effective, but that they were pleased with the volunteer himself— "pleased with me." Some congregations have "testimonies" during a worship service, articles in the church newsletter, or sharing during a midweek Bible study or prayer time. Again, the sharing of stories not only garners a continued stream of support for the service project, but it also provides indirect affirmation of volunteers.

Reflection on service and faith

Leaders support volunteers by encouraging them to reflect on why they serve. One pastor keeps reminding his volunteers that they serve in order to honor God, whether or not they see any immediate results of their service. He believes that when volunteers can be encouraged to keep on even when their service leads to disappointment, it strengthens their faith. In fact, seeing the fruit of service is "gravy on the biscuit," or icing on the cake, depending on your culinary culture.[11] He went on to say that as they went into the fiery furnace, Shadrach, Meshach, and Abednego knew God was able to deliver them, but they did not know if God would (Daniel 3). Whether they were killed or not, "God would still be God." The pastor summed up that if their church serves for twenty years and sees no results, that should not change their commitment. They serve because they honor God by serving. Volunteers need to be called back again and again to this foundation for their service.

Like the pastor's connecting the discouragement that comes in serving to the story from Daniel, leaders facilitate reflection by connecting service experiences with Scriptures and conversations about faith. Another pastor described meeting with adolescents after a service project to ask them, "Where did you experience God in your work?" Providing structured time for reflection is important for adults as well. Later in the chapter, we will explore further how to make the connection between service and faith strong and deep.

Prayer support

Ongoing congregational prayer support is critical for community ministry. Henri Nouwen notes that we can do hard things, overcome obstacles, and persevere under pressure and through disappointments, but when we no longer experience ourselves as part of a caring, supporting, praying community, we quickly lose faith. Faith in God's compassionate presence cannot be separated from experiencing God's presence in the community to which we belong, and that experience comes from praying together.[12] Prayer needs to be part of every service team, including family teams. And prayer for the service and those who serve also needs to be part of the larger community's life together.

Welcoming culture

Congregations need to be ready to welcome the service recipients if they want to become a part of the congregation. A perceived rejection of the recipients is a rejection of the ministry itself—and of the volunteers. In our research, several volunteers reported that they were dismayed that when they tried to include service recipients in congregational activities, the visitors were not welcomed. A tutor in a neighborhood elementary school was deeply angry and hurt when children from the school began attending the congregation's activities and a couple of families left the congregation because they did not want their children to be in the same activity programs with the children from impoverished families of a different ethnic heritage. In another congregation, members were upset when homeless men who were coming to the free lunch program also began coming to the Wednesday night church supper. "Those" men did not have the table manners or the clean apparel that some members thought were mandatory for joining in the church supper. Like the early church, too often we want to serve but we want to keep the people we are serving at a comfortable distance because they may create more problems if they come too close. Congregations, therefore, need to have conversations about their willingness to welcome before the service begins, as well as all along the way.

Ongoing planning

Ministry programs require considerable planning: planning the schedule for an inner-city children's activities program, organizing drivers for a meals-on-wheels program, or preparing lessons for an English as a Second Language program. Planning includes evaluating the impact of the program on volunteers as well as on the recipients, and sometimes changing direction if the program does not seem to be having the intended effects. It requires a careful balancing act and discernment. We do not stop programs because service recipients do not respond by changing their lives overnight or because they are not grateful. On the other hand, if it is clear that the work is not helping, perhaps even causing recipients to feel misunderstood and be treated condescendingly, then it is time to go back to the drawing board— or even better, to sit down with the recipients and learn from them what might be a more helpful approach. Too often congregations and their volunteers decide what they will do in service for others, without involving or consulting those being served.

Practice principle: Conduct an inventory of congregational life to determine if all of these ten community elements are in place. All ten elements do not necessarily need to be fully developed before the ministry begins, but the development of these elements, so vital for sustaining the ministry, deserves as rigorous a plan as the plan for implementing the service itself. Set a time periodically to review these ten elements to determine the extent that they are shaping the congregation's life together.

Becoming an Inside Out Congregation

We found that these ten elements that sustain a particular ministry also contribute to the development of an inside out culture in congregational life. Moreover, in the process of becoming inside out, congregations also develop closer ties within. Both pastors and volunteers described stronger relationships of members with one another. A retired Episcopalian widow who led her congregation's ministry advocating for international fair trade and environmentally sustainable practices told us that the committee moved from meeting once a month to twice a month because the committee wanted to become more of a community with one another. They are still the steering committee for their advocacy work, but they are also much more—they are friends and faith-family for one another. A pastor of another congregation said that the congregation's service to the poor of their community has resulted in cohesion, trust, and growth for the congregation itself; "it makes the community love on each other."

So, the cycle begins again, as figure 3 shows. Perhaps the most critical link in this cycle is the service-faith connection that happens in the preparation of volunteers before they serve and the conversation and reflection that takes place afterward. Yet our research shows that this is often the weakest link for many congregations. The congregation is more likely to publicize the ministry, take up an offering for it, and recognize the volunteers publicly than they are to guide the faith-service connection that is so vital.

Making the Service-Faith Connection

Our research focused on the relationship between service and the faith of volunteers, using the Faith Maturity Scale, an instrument developed by Peter Benson and his colleagues.[13] The scale assumes that faith grows and deepens over time as persons grow and mature. The scale has two dimensions: vertical and horizontal. The vertical dimension measures the person's relationship with God, and the horizontal dimension measures the person's relationship with others.

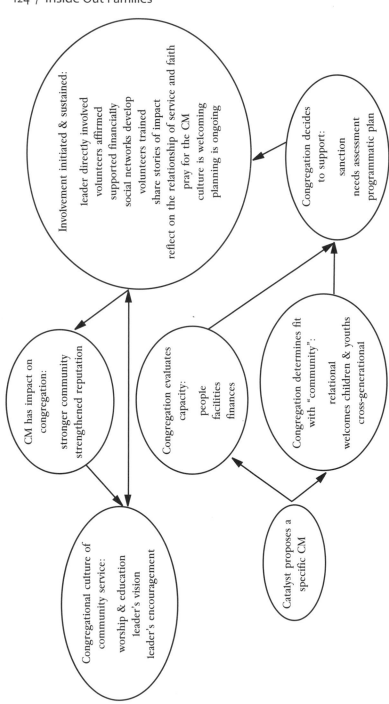

Figure 3—How congregations launch and sustain community ministries

In addition, based on the theoretical work of Dorothy Bass and Craig Dykstra, we developed the Christian Faith Practices Scale (CFPS) that included a list of thirteen faith behaviors or "practices" such as worship, hospitality, prayer, and Bible study.[14] Our research then determined how the items on the Faith Maturity Scale and the CFPS were related to the service experiences of congregants. We found several characteristics of the service experiences of these congregants that were powerfully and positively related to how "mature" their faith was, and the extent to which they engaged in the faith practices.[15]

Volunteers Receive the Preparation They Need for the Service

Volunteers need to understand the culture and needs of the recipients, lest they do more harm than good. Moreover, if volunteers are not prepared and the experience does not meet their expectations, the volunteers' stereotypes about persons who are economically poor and culturally different may be reinforced. Martha Stice, a social worker in a Baptist congregation in Texas, provides a great example of how to prepare volunteers for service. Her congregation was preparing to serve in a "Christmas toy store" through an inner-city agency. At this "store," parents living in poverty could choose a certain number of toys to purchase at greatly reduced prices to give to their children for Christmas. The toy store is an alternative to congregations giving Christmas toys directly to children. One of the greatest joys of parenthood is being able to give children gifts that they want. It is impoverishing and underscores the inadequacy of parents to have to stand by and watch someone else play Santa Claus for their children when they cannot. Allowing parents to give good gifts to their children is not as much fun for a volunteer as watching a child's face light up when the volunteer places a desired toy in the child's arms, but it is a more sensitive, loving, and empowering service to both child and parent and contributes to their relationship with one another.

It would be easy simply to allow volunteers to show up and serve: putting the toys out, greeting parents when they arrive and telling them how the store works, helping parents with toy selection, or running the checkout counter. Weeks before the actual day of the toy store, however, Martha prepared the following letter, which she sent to those who were preparing volunteers to serve, who in turn met with their groups before the service began to talk about their expectations and what they might experience:

> The Christmas Toy Store is just a little over two weeks away. As you organize your group of volunteers, I wanted to offer some questions and conversation topics to help prepare us all for the volunteer experience. An important part of serving others that is often overlooked is spiritually preparing ourselves for the experience and then reflecting back on what it meant to us afterwards. Read the following and prepare to discuss it with your group before you go to serve:
>
> *Putting Yourself in Their Place*
>
> The families we will be serving will be purchasing gifts for their children at very low costs. These parents are very aware that they are not shopping in a "real" store. Some may feel some embarrassment about that. Embarrassment often doesn't show as embarrassment, however. When people are embarrassed, sometimes it shows as anger—it's frustrating to be so poor that one has to take charity from others. Others may act "entitled" or proud to cover up their embarrassment. At the same time, many of these parents are dealing with many other stressful things in their lives (just as you might be). They may be having difficulty paying bills or paying for other necessities, or they may be worried about a job, have a sick child or car trouble, or be sick themselves.
>
> You are likely to experience many people grateful for your help and for these toys, but you will also likely encounter some parents that will snap at you and behave rudely. Remember that they don't really know you so their behavior is not really about you but really about how they are feeling and the stressors in their lives. Have patience; share joy. As Christians, caring for others is about how we treat them as an expression of our love for God, not how others treat us in return.

If you love those who love you, what credit is that to you? Even "sinners" love those who love them. And if you do good to those who are good to you, what credit is that to you? Even "sinners" do that. And if you lend to those from whom you expect repayment, what credit is that to you? Even "sinners" lend to "sinners," expecting to be repaid in full. But love your enemies, do good to them, and lend to them without expecting to get anything back. Then your reward will be great, and you will be sons of the Most High, because he is kind to the ungrateful and wicked. Be merciful, just as your father is merciful. (Luke 6:32-36 NIV)

Why are we doing this?

Why go through the difficulty and chaos of having a Toy Store? Why not just buy the presents and give them directly to the kids? The Toy Store is not only about making sure boys and girls have happy Christmases because they receive gifts, but it is a small way to help build stronger families. Allowing parents to pick out toys for their children shows respect to the parents. It shows them that we believe they know what is best for their own children. Asking parents to pay something for these toys allows them to take pride and ownership in what they are giving to their children. We are supporting parents' ability to show love and care for their children. In turn, children learn to turn to their own parents for support and believe in their parents' ability to care for them.

Questions to discuss with your group *before* serving in the store:

1. What are your expectations for serving at the Toy Store?
2. What kind of responses do you expect from the people you will serve?
3. What is your motivation for serving at the Toy Store?

Questions to discuss with your group *after* serving in the store:

1. How did the reality of your volunteering experience differ from your expectation? How was it the same?

2. What was the best part of your volunteering experience?
   Where did you see Jesus today?
3. What kinds of needs did you see today that your family or
   our congregation could work to address?

Martha Stice prepared the volunteers of her congregation not just to
serve, but to have compassion for those they served.

Robert Wuthnow conducted extensive research to understand
how people develop and sustain compassion for others. He notes that
we develop stories to explain our service.[16] Telling stories about our
experiences enables us to explain the meaning it has for us. Sarah
Hall told the story of going with her family to the inner-city children's recreational program when she was eight. She captured the
meaning of the service for her own faith, when she said,

> I've grown up in a family where we've always gone to church. I
> have always known about Jesus and we always pray, so that's not
> new to me. But going to Calvary, I met kids who didn't know
> about Jesus Christ, and it made me not want to take my faith for
> granted. I hope by the way I acted they could feel God's love.

The time for reflection together should wrap volunteer service with
specific prayer for the work and for those served, and with Bible
study related to the work. The interlocking combination of service,
Bible study, reflection, and prayer is Christian education at its best.

The Service Experience Provides Opportunity for a Relationship
to Grow between Those Serving and Those Served

Habitat for Humanity requires that every family for whom they build
a home contribute "sweat equity." Not only does their involvement in
construction underscore that they are not just passive recipients but
have an investment in the new home, it also enables the volunteers
to put faces to the family they are serving. It was so meaningful and
powerful for my family to come to know one other family well and
to struggle with how together we could help their children succeed
in school and the parents find steady jobs with livable wages—more
than if we had raised money for the homeless family shelter or served

a meal there. In turn, however, the raising of money or other less relational opportunities became more meaningful when we knew at least one family who would have benefited from our work.

The Service Involves Doing with Recipients, Not Doing for Them

Too often, service is planned without any input from those the service is supposedly going to help. At the beginning of my social work career, I served as the social worker in a Baptist children's home, where we cared for children whose families could not provide adequate care. We would get shipments of diapers from well-meaning folks who wanted to help "those poor orphans." In fact, we had no children under age twelve; younger children were placed in foster care. Our older children and teenagers could have really benefited from families befriending them, helping with school supplies and clothes, and buying a prom dress or renting a tux so they could go to their senior prom like all the other graduates. But most people did not ask; they just assumed. Although their assumptions wasted resources, they really did not do much harm other than being useless.

Unfortunately, volunteers can do real harm by assuming they know the needs of others and proceeding on that assumption. Jim Dekker has pointed out that when we talk to people who are serving, we may hear of self-sacrifice and compassionate care. But if we ask those served, we might hear that volunteers were condescending. Those served may feel like objects rather than persons with interesting lives and gifts themselves to offer. Those serving may think that they are forming relationships, but those served may feel like the local people in another culture who are being photographed by tourists.[17]

More than finding out from the people served what they perceive to be their needs, it is even more helpful to serve *with, alongside* them. Perhaps the most important goal of the relationship between the "server" and the "recipient" is that their relationship becomes mutual—both are serving, both are receiving. Susan Crismon learned that the children in her home in the afterschool hours could help her with some of her chores as well as her helping them with their homework. It was important for her to accept small gifts and care from the families whose children she was providing care. The best hospitality works itself out of being hospitality because the relationship becomes increasingly mutual, increasingly family. This kind of service takes time, because the focus is forming a relationship, not doing a project. Volunteers and service recipients are no longer volunteers and service recipients; they are not "haves" and "have nots"; they are people trying to care for one another in helpful, sensitive ways.

Unfortunately, we could not determine if serving *with* rather than *for* had any impact on the faith of the volunteers in the congregations we studied, because very few volunteers were working in settings that actually included the service recipients in the planning and in the activity. That was a sobering finding.

Working with Persons Who Are Different from Volunteers in Some Significant Way Can Stretch the Volunteers into Deeper Empathy and Compassion

It may be relatively easy and comfortable for me to tutor a child who looks like and talks like my own children, but I will not be much challenged or changed by the experience. If that child stretches me to relate to her because English is not her first language and I do not speak Spanish, and she relates to adults differently than my children do because she has a different cultural background, and her views of the world and how things work are very different from mine—I am going to end up stretched and changed. I will learn about her, and about me, and my views on the world will most likely change as I struggle to understand what it looks like through her eyes. There are many, many ways that people are different from one another: age, income, poverty, ethnicity, language, religious beliefs, sexual orientation, worldviews, and life circumstances. The more different we are, the more challenging it is to relate to one another, and the more our worlds will be changed if we can hang in there and learn to care for one another. The challenge to the church leader is to connect servants and recipients who share enough in common that they can communicate with one another, and who are different enough that both learn a deeper compassion for others.

*Volunteers Work through the Inevitable Conflicts That Develop
Rather Than Quitting*

Inevitably, volunteers will face conflict, whether it is disagreement with other volunteers or the service recipients about the task, or about values, or about any of the other issues over which people conflict. Sometimes people have a hard time liking one another and they assume liking is a prerequisite for serving or loving others. It is not. Family members sometimes run into spells during which they do not like one another very much, and they grow as a family when they hang together through those times because they love one another. We grow in faith and in love when we work it through.

Anger is a God-given emotional signaling device, designed to alert us that something is wrong. It is to relationships with others what pain is to the physical body. Pain beginning in the chest and running down the arm is an important signal of a potentially dangerous problem that needs to be attended to immediately. Even if the pain dissolves for a time, to ignore it is to put the body in peril. Anger is relationship pain. It indicates that there is a problem somewhere in the relationship that needs to be corrected, if possible. It needs to be reported to one another in ways that truthfully name the problem (Eph 4:25), in ways that do not lead to sin against one another (Eph 4:26) and that build up rather than tear down the other and the relationship (Eph 4:29). Truthfully naming the problem means reporting one's experience and feelings, such as, "I am upset because you did not show up and I was expecting you," not naming the other in ways that tear the other down and thus sin against the other: "You are so unreliable; I just can't depend on you."

The teachings of Jesus make clear that no matter where the problem originates, we have a responsibility to tackle it. In Matthew 5:23-24, self is the offending party: "So when you are offering your gift at the altar, if you remember that your brother or sister has something against you, leave your gift there before the altar and go; first be reconciled to your brother or sister, and then come and offer your gift." In Matthew 18:15, the other person is the offending party. "If another member of the church sins against you, go and point out the fault when the two of you are alone. If the member listens to you, you have regained that one." In both situations, the instruction is to go and establish a communication link, regardless of whether one is the culprit or the victim.[18]

One Scripture passage has created particular difficulties for some Christians. Ephesians 4:26 says, "Be angry but do not sin; do not let the sun go down on your anger." It recognizes the importance of anger but also cautions that it can easily lead to sin. Unfortunately, this verse has often been paraphrased, "Do not go to bed angry." The new day for Jews began at sunset, not in the morning, as in our culture. Paul is thus saying that anger should not be allowed to go on into the new day that began at sundown. Or we might say, anger should not infect our "tomorrows" with one another. Christians should not allow anger to fester unaddressed. They should avoid allowing anger at others to take up permanent residence in their hearts, destroying relationships.

In Ephesians 4:29, Paul writes, "Let no evil talk come out of your mouths, but only what is useful for building up, as there is need, so that your words may give grace to those who hear." Reporting anger, then, means saying or doing what *needs* to be said or done in order to bring grace to the hearer. That is, the anger is *used* in behalf of the relationship. Anger is used to *build up* the relationship by tackling issues and problems together. It is *not* using anger to prove self as right, wonderful, and long-suffering, and others as wrong, terrible, and mean-spirited. It is certainly not used to bolster one's self-esteem at the expense of others. When the expression of anger is designed to build up one's self, then one has not really taken to heart the good news of the gospel.

Working with others will lead to conflict, and conflict leads to anger. Therefore, the service together provides a grand opportunity for discipling Christians to use the anger in behalf of our relationships and the work to which we are called. If we can learn to handle conflict constructively in the community of faith, it can carry over to how families handle conflict at home and, with grace and blessing, even to church business meetings and deacon business councils.

The Volunteers Feel Challenged, and Their Gifts Are Used Well

Service opportunities are not "one size fits all." Some people enjoy the challenge of building relationships with other volunteers and the community guests in a soup kitchen, finding it deeply satisfying to feed those who otherwise would go hungry—ladling beef stew into paper bowls and placing corn bread on top. Others may be frustrated by the experience, realizing that in four hours the people they are serving will be hungry again, and then, there may not be a free meal. Instead, they would be better challenged and sense that their time was being better used in developing a community business, where the guests of the soup kitchen can be offered jobs and partial business ownership with incomes so they can purchase their own food.[19] Both are valuable. The challenge to church leaders is to match the gifts and callings of congregants and their families with the opportunities for service and community action all around.

Leaders need to be helping families not only to serve needs but also to advocate for justice. Serving beef stew for six months may be deeply satisfying and fills an important need, but as time goes by, leaders can challenge volunteers to think about and consider how they can tackle the systems and powers that create hunger and homelessness. When people are drowning, it is critical that we jump into the river and pull them out. But when screaming people keep floating downstream needing to be rescued, it is time to go see who is throwing them in and put a stop to it.

Anne Davis points out that priests were those individuals who carried the message of the people to God and that prophets brought God's message to the people.[20] From these two different roles there have emerged two different kinds of helping, the priestly and the prophetic. Priestly helping takes place in relationships between servant and recipient—service. Prophetic helping seeks social justice and social change directed at the larger, oppressing systems of society; it goes upstream to address the problems that are throwing people in the river. Jesus modeled both priestly and prophetic helping, loving kindness and seeking justice.

Leaders Make Time after the Service Experience
for Reflection and Conversation

Perhaps the most important aspect of service is the time for volunteers to think about and talk with their family and others about what they have experienced. Was the experience what I expected? Were the people I met like the picture I had? What did I learn from them? What did I learn about their lives, and about our society and world? How does this experience fit with my understanding of God and of myself? What needs to happen next? The questions Martha Stice placed at the end of her letter are good examples. People who are action-oriented and busy, however, often will skip on to the next activity unless the time for reflection and conversation is structured into the experience. Church leaders can make the time and space and be available for this reflection and conversation.

Volunteers need to hear the theological foundations for faith that are expressed through service, and have the opportunity to talk about their volunteer experiences in light of their faith. In its research with congregations engaged in community ministry, the Search Institute found that the deepest learning takes place when service is partnered with religious reflection and study of the meaning of the service.[21] Dieter Hessel has said that congregations are schools of Christian living that teach by doing mission/ministry and then reflecting in the context of Christian faith on those experiences.[22]

John Dewey and other advocates of experiential learning in educational settings have long recognized the importance of integrating service into learning experiences.[23] The process has been characterized as a hermeneutical cycle of learning.[24] Volunteers come to the service experience with their own values, beliefs, and skills based on their life experiences. But as they engage in service, particularly through developing relationships with persons in life circumstances radically different from their own, they experience dissonance with their initial values and beliefs, and feel the need for new skills. The service experience challenges the servants' understanding of how the world works, about what causes social problems such as poverty, homelessness, illness, school failure or whatever the problems are with which service recipients are struggling. As servants form relationships with the service recipients, they begin to see the complexity of recipients' lives and even how the world looks through those recipients' eyes.

The following four aspects of service experiences can provide a starting place for reflective conversation:

> *Stories about what they are learning and about the people with whom they work.* Reflection begins with remembering the experience. As we talk through what happened, we can help one another develop fresh perspectives and a compassion for those we are serving with and serving.

> *How their service is having an impact on their relationship with God.* Hearing others discuss this dimension of service may open volunteers to a deepened awareness of divine presence in their service. Simply asking the question, "How have you felt God's presence?" may provide an opportunity for telling stories about experiences that underscore their significance.

> *The impact service is having on their families and congregation.* In addition to the direct results of serving together, indirect results of service such as the development of tolerance and compassion may have influence in their family and community relationships.

> *The meaning of success.* Religious beliefs, values, and biblical texts can provide fodder for conversation about what success in service looks like for people of faith. Some interesting themes include whether God's kingdom breaks in or we bring it in through our work; and how God responds to our failures and what that means for our response to one another.

When to Keep On and When to Move On

Rusaw and Swanson have said that ministries that do not measure can neither rest nor worship.[25] They wisely see in a story about King Hezekiah a truth about community ministry. When Hezekiah became king of Judah, one of his first acts took great courage; he broke into pieces the bronze snake of Moses (2 Kgs 18:4b). During a plague of venomous snakes, Moses had fashioned the bronze snake so that if a snake bit anyone, they could look at Moses' bronze snake and live (Num 21:6-9). Generations had gone by, and the tool Moses fashioned had become an idol. The people were burning incense to the bronze snake—worshipping it rather than the God who gave the tool its original power. Congregations have a very hard time smashing revered programs; "We've always done it this way" is a mantra. Community ministries are tools used to deliver the love of God through the lives of servants. But they are only tools. There come times to leave one tool behind and pick up another.

Congregations can only know when it is time to abandon a ministry if they are measuring its impact. What difference is it making in the life of those it is intended to serve? What impact is it having on the faith of the families serving? What have we learned that suggests other tools to fashion? Have we served enough beef stew to be ready to tackle the issue of why all these people have to stand in line in our fellowship hall, week after week, to get a paper bowl of stew and act grateful for it? Is it time to proclaim Jubilee? What does proclaiming Jubilee look like in our neighborhood?

Notes

Introduction

1 In case you are curious about what happened to that rebellious fourteen-year-old now grown up, she is a journalist and has published her first book about some of the most marginalized persons in our society. She writes about immigrant children who grow up in a disturbing cycle of poverty in which their families, fleeing from troubled Central American cities, move into America's suburbs, only to find the patterns of gangs and violence repeating themselves. The book is *Gangs in Garden City: How Immigration, Segregation, and Youth Violence are Changing America's Suburbs* (New York: Nation Books, 2009).

2 For an extensive discussion of sociological and theological definitions of family, see Diana R. Garland, *Family Ministry: A Comprehensive Guide* (Grand Rapids: InterVarsity, 1999).

3 Ernest Burgess, "The Family as a Unity of Interacting Personalities," *The Family* 7, no. 1 (1926): 3–9.

4 All names of families and individuals we interviewed have been changed to protect their privacy.

5 This discussion of Jesus' teaching about family is excerpted from *Family Ministry: A Comprehensive Guide.* If you are intrigued, you may want to read more in chapter 1 of that volume.

6 Gilbert Meilaender, "A Christian View of the Family," in *Rebuilding the Nest: A New Commitment to the American Family*, ed. David

Blankenhorn, Steven Bayme, and Jean Bethke Elshtain (Milwaukee: Family Service America, 1990), 133–47.

7 Diana R. Garland, "'Who Is Your Family?' Membership Composition of American Protestant Families," *Social Work & Christianity* 29, no. 3 (2002): 183–223; idem, "The Church Census: A Congregational Assessment Tool for Family Ministry," *Family Ministry: Empowering through Faith* 18, no. 1 (2004): 46–61; idem, "The Families in Our Congregations: Initial Research Findings," *Family Ministry: Empowering through Faith* 18, no. 1 (2004): 62–87; Diana R. Garland and Jo A. Edmonds, "Family Life of Baptists," *Family and Community Ministries: Empowering through Faith* 21, no. 1 (2007): 6–21; Diana R. Garland and Pamela Yankeelov, "The Church Census," *Family Ministry: Empowering through Faith* 12, no. 3 (1998): 11–22; idem, "The Strengths, Stresses and Faith Practices of Congregational Families," *Family Ministry: Empowering through Faith* 15, no. 3 (2001): 28–47.

8 See also Diana R. Garland, "Faith Narratives of Congregants and Their Families," *Review of Religious Research* 44, no. 1 (2002): 68–91; idem, "Families and Their Faith," in *Christianity and Social Work: Readings on the Integration of Christian Faith and Social Work Practice*, ed. Beryl Hugen and T. Laine Scales (Botsford, Conn.: NACSW, 2002), 119–43; idem, "Family Stories: Resources for Nurturing Family Faith in Congregational Life," *Family Ministry: Empowering through Faith* 18, no. 3 (2004): 26–44; and idem, "The Sacred in Family Stories," *Family Ministry: Empowering through Faith* 19, no. 2 (2005): 41–60.

9 This project has been reported in the following academic journal articles: Diana R. Garland, et al., "Effective Leadership of Faith-Motivated Volunteers in Community Service Programs" (paper presented at the Annual Program Meeting of the Council on Social Work Education, Nashville, Tenn., February 2002); Diana R. Garland, Dennis Myers, and Terry A. Wolfer, "The Impact of Volunteering on Christian Faith and Congregational Life: The Service and Faith Project," Baylor University, http://www.baylor.edu/~CFCM/; Diana R. Garland, Dennis M. Myers, and Terry A. Wolfer, "Learning to See People as God Sees Them: Outcomes of Community Service for Congregational Volunteers," *Review of Religious Research* (forthcoming); S. Denise Abbott, et al., "Social Workers' Views of Local Churches as Service Providers: Impressions from an Exploratory Study," *Social Work & Christianity* 17 (1990): 7–16; Michael E. Sherr, Diana Garland, and Terry Wolfer, "The Role of Community Service in the Faith Development of Adolescents," *The Journal of Youth Ministry* 6, no. 1 (2007): 43–54.

10 Eric Swanson coined the term "sticky faith" when pondering with me this finding of the Service and Faith Project.

Chapter 1

1 I first told this story in my book *Sacred Stories of Ordinary Families: Living the Faith in Daily Life* (San Francisco: Jossey-Bass, 2003).

2 Ten congregations in each denomination in each region were selected randomly from a list of congregations provided by the regional denominational office. From these ten congregations, the two participating congregations were selected that differed from each other and from other churches already in the sample as much as possible on the following variables: size of the congregation, location (inner city, urban, suburban), and theological position (conservatism/liberalism) relative to other congregations in their denomination. Once congregations had been selected, I contacted the pastor to determine the congregation's willingness to participate. When a congregation chose not to participate, the next congregation in the listing that provided significant diversity on salient dimensions was chosen. In every case, this third congregation agreed to participate when one of the first two did not. Those congregations that chose not to participate did so because they were in the midst of major transitions in congregational life, such as a change in pastors or a crisis of one kind or another.

3 Most of the interviews were conducted in the midwestern and southern urban areas selected for the project. The families represented the following regions: South (n=52), Midwest (n=51), Southwest (n=5), and Pacific Northwest (n=2). They represented their denominations as follows: Southern Baptists (n=34), Presbyterians (n=22), National Baptists (n=19), and United Methodists (n=35).

4 The resulting sample of families interviewed included cohabiting heterosexual couples (n=5) roommates of the same gender (n=1), single parents and their children (n=11), adult siblings (n=2), an elderly parent and grown children (n=3), and single adults alone (n=13). The sample also included married couples with (n=48) and without (n=26) children, and in first (n=54) and second or later (n=20) marriages. Many families included other assorted relatives and nonrelatives: exchange students, foster children, nieces and nephews, grandchildren, and close friends (n=16). An average of 2.47 persons was present in each interview, with a range of 1 to 6 persons.

5 Interviews were tape recorded and transcribed in full. The interview questions gave minimal structure to the interview. I followed the family's leading for the order of the discussion rather than the ordering of the questions, simply making sure by the end of the interview that all questions had been addressed at some point. After leaving the family home, I dictated for transcription my observations of the family and their home and neighborhood, the process and nonverbal processes of the interview,

and any impressions of the family and the interview I wanted to remember. The interview questions changed over the process of the research, in response to what I was learning. The final questions were:

1. Adults: tell me about your families growing up, and how this family group got started.
2. Children: What are your first memories of this family? What happened after that?
3. Tell me about a typical day in your family now. A typical week.
4. Tell me about something in your family's life—big or small—that pictures your family at its best.
5. What is most important for your family currently? What do you give a lot of attention to?
6. What gives your life together purpose and meaning? Tell me a story about that.
7. What are your family goals and dreams?
8. What does the word "faith" mean to you? (ask each family member)
9. When have you felt God especially close to your family? (ask for illustration)
10. When have you experienced God's absence in your family's life? (ask for illustration)
11. In what ways has your faith been influenced by living in this family? (both ways it has been strengthened and ways it may have been challenged or diminished)
12. Are there things you do together regularly—rituals or habits you share—that express your values as a family?
13. How has the role of faith in your life together changed over time, or has it?
14. Are there ways you nurture your faith together, or does it just happen as a part of living?
15. What help do you get from outside your family in living out your commitments and faith?
16. What interferes with your family's ability to live out its commitments and faith? Are these different for different family members?
17. What might help you as a family to live your faith together?
18. Tell me a favorite Bible story. What about this story speaks to you?

6 I coded the database, using a system that grew to more than three hundred codes throughout the analysis and that combined both content themes and interactional processes. The analysis developed following a grounded theory approach. See Kathy Charmaz, *Constructing*

Grounded Theory: A Practical Guide through Qualitative Analysis (London: Sage, 2006); Anselm Strauss and Juliet Corbin, *Basics of Qualitative Research: Techniques and Procedures for Developing Grounded Theory*, 2nd ed. (Thousand Oaks: Sage, 1998); and Robert S. Weiss, *Learning from Strangers: The Art and Method of Qualitative Interview Studies* (New York: Free Press, 1994).

7   I also recorded and transcribed these focus groups.

8   Fowler's work on the stages of faith development can be found in the following publications: James W. Fowler, *Becoming Adult, Becoming Christian* (San Francisco: Jossey-Bass, 2000); idem, "Faith and the Structuring of Meaning," in *Faith Development and Fowler*, ed. Craig Dykstra and Sharon Parks (Birmingham, Ala.: Religious Education Press, 1986), 15–42; idem, "Faith Development through the Family Life Cycle," in *Catholic Families: Growing and Sharing Faith* (New Rochelle, N.Y.: Don Bosco Multimedia, 1990), 98–116; idem, *Stages of Faith: The Psychology of Human Development and the Quest for Meaning* (San Francisco: Harper & Row, 1981); idem, *Weaving the New Creation: Stages of Faith and the Public Church* (San Francisco: Harper, 1991).

9   The following publications explore faith as activity or "practice": Dorothy C. Bass and Craig Dykstra, "Growing in the Practices of Faith," in *Practicing Our Faith: A Way of Life for a Searching People*, ed. Dorothy C. Bass (San Francisco: Jossey-Bass, 1997), 195–204; Craig Dykstra, *Growing in the Life of Faith: Education and Christian Practices* (Louisville, Ky.: Geneva Press, 1999); idem, "Reconceiving Practice," in *Shifting Boundaries: Contextual Approaches to the Structure of Theological Education*, ed. Barbara Wheeler and Edward Farley (Louisville, Ky.: Westminster John Knox, 1991), 37–55; and idem, "What Is Faith?: An Experiment in the Hypothetical Mode," in Dykstra and Parks, *Faith Development*, 45–64.

10   H. I. McCubbin, M. A. McCubbin, and A. I. Thompson, "Resiliency in Families: The Role of Family Schema and Appraisal in Family Adaptation to Crises," in *Family Relations: Challenges for the Future*, ed. T. H. Brubaker (Newbury Park, Calif.: Sage, 1993), 154. See also Hamilton I. McCubbin and Charles R. Figley, "Bridging Normative and Catastrophic Family Stress," in *Stress and the Family, vol. 1: Coping with Normative Transitions*, ed. McCubbin and Figley (New York: Brunner/Mazel, 1983), 218–28; Hamilton I. McCubbin and Marilyn A. McCubbin, "Resilient Families, Competencies, Supports, and Coping over the Life Cycle," in *Faith and Families*, ed. Lindell Sawyers (Philadelphia: Geneva Press, 1986), 65–88.

11 Nora Gallagher, *Practicing Resurrection* (New York: Alfred A. Knopf, 2003), 3.

12 I first explored the concept of faith as melody in *Sacred Stories of Ordinary Families*, the full report of the Families and Faith Project.

13 For an exploration of these stories, see David E. Garland and Diana R. Garland, *Flawed Families of the Bible: How God Works through Imperfect Relationships* (Grand Rapids: Brazos Press, 2007).

14 The Church Census is available from the Center for Family and Community Ministries, Baylor School of Social Work, P.O. Box 97320, One Bear Place, Waco, TX 76798-7320, or 254-710-6400.

15 See Garland and Edmonds, "Family Life of Baptists"; Garland, "Church Census"; idem, "The Families in Our Congregations"; and idem, "'Who Is Your Family?'"

16 The list "How the church can help" now contains the following items:

Family Home Life
Communication skills
Understanding personality differences
Handling conflict and anger
Romance and sexuality in marriage
Romance and sexuality in single life
Guiding children and teens in learning about sexuality
Disciplining children
Male and female roles
Developing family traditions
Balancing privacy and togetherness
Managing time
Managing money
Working out chores and family responsibilities
Confessing, forgiving, reconciling after hurt
Talking about our faith together
Family prayer and devotional time
Family Bible study
Developing healthy habits—eating, exercise, rest & recreation
Opportunities for children to interact with positive adult role models

Specific Challenges
Caring for sick, disabled, or aging family members
Death and grief
Coping with crises
Building friendships as a family
Relating to television and other media
Retirement

Drug and alcohol abuse
Depression, mental illness
Sexual/physical/emotional abuse, past or present
Sexual orientation
Death and grief
Interfaith families
Problem pregnancy

Family on Mission
Caring for God's created world as a family
Working as a family for more justice in the world
Knowing what we can do together to make a difference for others
Finding ways we can include all ages in community service
Connecting community service to our faith
Sharing service opportunities with other families in the congregation

Family Stages
Dating and romantic relationships
Relating to roommates, adult siblings
Preparing for marriage
Divorce—before, during, and after
Remarriage and forming stepfamilies
Developing a strong marriage
Parenting infants and preschoolers
Parenting school-age children
Parenting teenagers
Parent–young adult–child relationships
Grandparents raising children
Single parenting
Middle age/senior adult family relationships
Retirement

17 This finding was reported in the article Garland and Edmonds, "Family Life of Baptists." As a consequence of this finding, we have expanded this section of the survey to include the six items listed above in the section of the Church Census called "Family on Mission."

18 This scale has become the Christian Faith Practices Scale and is available in Michael Sherr, James Stamey, and Diana R. Garland, "Empowering Faith Practices: A Validation Study of the Christian Faith Practices Scale," *Journal of Family and Community Ministries* 23, no. 1 (2009): 27–35.

19 I am grateful to my colleagues in the Service and Faith project: Dennis Myers, Terry Wolfer, Michael Sherr, David Sherwood, Paula Sheridan, Beryl Hugen, Scott Taylor, and Kelly Atkinson. All of us are grateful to

Lilly Endowment, Inc., for providing funding for the Service and Faith project.

20 The research team chose a purposive sample of thirty-five Protestant Christian congregations located in four areas of the United States—the Upper Midwest (n=8), the South (n=8), the Southwest (n=13), and Southern California (n=6). The congregations were Evangelical Protestant (n=22) (e.g., Southern Baptist, Cooperative Baptist Fellowship, Missionary Baptist, Seventh-day Adventist, Christian Reformed, Assemblies of God, and "nondenominational") and mainline Protestant (n=13) (e.g., United Methodist, Presbyterian USA, and Episcopal). The sample of activist congregations was selected based on their reputation among religious leaders in each region for being involved in community ministry. These religious leaders nominated congregations based on their knowledge of the most active congregations. The team then selected congregations that represented the most theological and ethnic diversity to the array of congregations in the sample.

The research team defined community ministry as involvement in activities encouraged by the church that support the physical, material, emotional, and social well-being of people from the congregation, neighborhood, or community. Those activities could take place through congregational programs or through community organizations. This definition of community ministry does not include acts of kindness or charity that take place in informal human interaction. All the congregations in this study were involved in at least one form of community ministry. In other words, not only were their members involved personally as volunteers, but the congregation itself had a formal commitment either to offer a program of community service or to collaborate with other community service organizations.

The research team members conducted surveys of congregational attendees, both those who were actively volunteering in the community and those who were not. The analysis of findings from the thirty-five congregations is based on the 7,403 responses to a congregational survey and 946 responses to a volunteer survey. Nearly half of the respondents (46.5%, n=3,442) reported personal involvement in community service activities. In addition to the surveys, in all four regions the research team conducted in-depth interviews lasting from one to two hours each with twenty-nine congregational leaders, twenty-five individual volunteers and an additional sixteen families who were actively involved together in community service programs. Congregation leaders identified the families and individuals for interview.

Chapter 2

1   See Peter Benson, Michael J. Donahue, and Joseph A. Erickson, "The Faith Maturity Scale: Conceptualization, Measurement, and Empirical Validation," *Research in the Social Scientific Study of Religion* 5 (1993): 1–26. A summary of our research on the social scientific study of faith, including instruments for measuring faith, can be found in Beryl Hugen, Terry A. Wolfer, and Jennifer Ubels Renkema, "Service and Faith: The Impact on Faith of Community Ministry Participation," *Review of Religious Research* 47, no. 4 (2006): 409–26. See also Dennis R. Myers, Terry A. Wolfer, and Diana R. Garland, "Congregational Service-Learning Characteristics and Volunteer Faith Development," *Religious Education* 103, no. 3 (2008): 369–86. The most prominent scale being used to study faith is the Faith Maturity Scale. This scale defines the core dimensions of faith as the *vertical*, or the personal transformation one experiences in the divine encounter, and the *horizontal*, or heeding the call to social service and social justice. Examples of items from the horizontal dimension include: "In my free time, I help people with problems or needs"; "I am active in efforts to promote social justice"; "I feel a deep sense of responsibility for reducing pain and suffering in the world"; and "I give significant portions of time and money to help other people." The survey instrument asks respondents to indicate how often they participate in these behaviors on a seven-point Likert scale ranging from "never" to "always." With permission of the authors, we used the short version of the Faith Maturity Scale in our surveys of congregations. See also R. L. Piedmont and R. Nelson, "A Psychometric Evaluation of the Short Form of the Faith Maturity Scale," *Social Scientific Study of Religion* 12 (2001): 165–83.

2   Dieter T. Hessel, *Social Ministry* (Philadelphia: Westminster Press, 1982), 110. See also idem, *Social Ministry*, rev. ed. (Philadelphia: Westminster Press, 1992).

3   Some of the most thoughtful discussions of the connection between the life of faith and ministry beyond the church include the following: Nancy T. Ammerman, *Pillars of Faith: American Congregations and Their Partners* (Berkeley: University of California Press, 2005); Andrew Billingsley, *Mighty Like a River: The Black Church and Social Reform* (New York: Oxford University Press, 1999); Harvie M. Conn, "Christian Social Ministry: What's the Problem?" *Urban Mission* 14, no. 1 (1996): 6–18; David W. Crocker, *Operation Inasmuch: Mobilizing Believers Beyond the Walls of the Church* (St. Louis, Mo.: Lake Hickory Resources, 2005); Carl S. Dudley, *Basic Steps toward Community Ministry* (Washington, D.C.: The Alban Institute, 1991); idem, *Next*

Steps in Community Ministry (Washington, D.C.: The Alban Institute, 1996); Roger L. Dudley, "Growing Faith," in *Valuegenesis: Faith in the Balance* (Riverside, Calif.: La Sierra University Press, 1992), 57–80; Kenneth L. Hall, *Inside Outside: The Church in Social Ministry* (Dallas: Family Matters Ministry of the Buckner Foundation, 1997); Hessel, *Social Ministry*, rev. ed.; Nancy T. Kinney and Mary L. Carver, "Urban Congregations as Incubators of Service Organizations," in *34th Annual Conference of the Association for Research on Nonprofit Organizations and Voluntary Action (ARNOVA)* (Washington, D.C., 2005); M. C. Nelson, "Why Do They Do It? A Study of Volunteer Commitment in the Parish Setting," *Journal of Volunteer Administration* 17, no. 2 (1999): 30–37; Rick Rusaw and Eric Swanson, *The Externally Focused Church* (Loveland, Colo.: Group, 2004); Heidi Rolland Unruhr, "Mobilizing and Equipping Your Church for Holistic Ministry," (paper presented at Conference on Working Together to Serve the Needy: Welfare Reform and the Faith Communities in Greater Philadelphia, Philadelphia, Pa., December 8, 1998); Derrell E. Watkins, *Christian Social Ministry: An Introduction* (Nashville: Broadman & Holman, 1994).

4   Alexander McElway, "The Systematic Theology of Faith: A Protestant Perspective," in *Handbook of Faith*, ed. James Michael Lee (Birmingham, Ala.: Religious Education Press, 1990), 164–200.

5   For a description of the early church's involvement in charity, see Luke Timothy Johnson, *The Acts of the Apostles*, ed. Daniel J. Harrington (Collegeville, Minn.: The Liturgical Press, 1992).

6   Marianne Sawicki opened my eyes to the story of Stephen in her article "Recognizing the Risen Lord," *Theology Today* 44, no. 4 (1988): 441–49.

7   Eelibuj is an invented word. Enjoy saying it the next time you want to respond with an expletive to a politician giving a speech on television.

8   Robert Coles, "The Profile of Spirituality of At-Risk Youth," in *The Ongoing Journey: Awakening Spiritual Life in At-Risk Youth*, ed. Terry Hyland and Ron Herron (Boys Town, Neb.: Boys Town Press, 1995), 7–35.

9   This project is described in note 14 in chapter 1. Interview transcripts were analyzed to develop theory grounded in the experiences of the interviewees as they told them to us (e.g., Weiss, *Learning from Strangers*). In the stories about these congregations and their members told in this book, identifying information has been changed to protect privacy. Interview transcripts have been edited to make them more readable while also preserving the meaning and voice of the interviewees.

10   This research is reported in the following publications: Eugene Roehlkepartain, "What Makes Faith Mature?" *Christian Century* 107, no. 6

(1990): 496–99; Roehlkepartain, Elanah Dalyah Naftali, and Laura Musegades, *Growing up Generous: Engaging Youth in Giving and Serving* (Bethesda, Md.: Alban Institute, 2000); Roehlkepartain and Dorothy L. Williams, *Exploring Faith Maturity* (Minneapolis: Lutheran Brotherhood, 1990).

11 Roehlkepartain, Naftali, and Musegades, *Growing up Generous*, 21.

12 Christian Smith and Melinda Lundquist Denton, *Soul Searching: The Religious and Spiritual Lives of American Teeenagers* (New York: Oxford University Press, 2005), 69.

13 Mark Chaves, *Congregations in America* (Cambridge, Mass.: Harvard University Press, 2004), 50.

14 Rusaw and Swanson, *Externally Focused Church*, 16.

15 Rusaw and Swanson, *Externally Focused Church*, 88–89.

16 David Campbell and Steven Yonish also report that churchgoing families volunteer together. Their research found that the proportion of respondents reporting that they perform volunteer work as a family increases markedly as church attendance increases. David E. Campbell and Steven J. Yonish, "Religion and Volunteering in America," in *Religion as Social Capital: Producing the Common Good*, ed. Corwin Smidt (Waco, Tex.: Baylor University Press, 2003), 95.

17 Roehlkepartain, Naftali, and Musegades, *Growing up Generous*, 149.

18 Smith and Denton, *Soul Searching*, 261.

19 Smith and Denton, *Soul Searching*, 261.

20 Robert Wuthnow, *Learning to Care: Elementary Kindness in an Age of Indifference* (Princeton: Princeton University Press, 1995), 46.

21 Jack Calhoun, "Claiming Youth: A New Paradigm in Youth Policy," *New Directions for Philanthropic Fundraising* 38 (2002): 67–80.

Chapter 3

1 The suggestions in this chapter for engaging families in ministry are based on analysis of the interviews with individuals and families we conducted as part of the Service and Faith project, described in footnotes in chapter 1.

Chapter 4

1 I drew the challenges described in this section from my analysis of the interviews with families in the Service and Faith project. All of these families actually engaged for a year or more in community service. The challenges listed here are the most common across the different kinds of families and service engagement. It should certainly not be considered a comprehensive list for every family and situation.

Chapter 5

1 Songs stay in our heads for pondering like stories. For decades, Dr. Fred Rogers' children's show *Mister Rogers' Neighborhood* has been a staple in many homes with young children, including ours. The show began national distribution on PBS in 1968 and continued for thirty-three years. In 2000, the Religion Communicators Council gave Dr. Rogers the Lifetime Wilbur Award for supporting religious values in the public media. He began each show by walking onto the set as though he was coming home, changing into sneakers and a sweater, and singing his theme song, "Won't You Be My Neighbor?" To read the story of his life and contribution, see http://www.post-gazette.com/ae/20030228rogersae1p1.asp.

2 These altitudes are reported at http://www.eyeonisrael.com.

3 Anne Davis, *Come, Go with Me: Following Christ's Example of Ministry and Witness* (Birmingham, Ala.: Woman's Missionary Union, 1997).

4 Rusaw and Swanson, *Eternally Focused Church*, 30.

5 On the congregational survey of more than 7,000 congregants, almost half (46%) reported that they were currently involved in community ministry, and two-thirds of those have been involved in community ministry for more than five years. Those respondents who have been involved in community ministry for six or more years had a significantly higher ($p \leq .01$) overall mean score on the Practices of Christian Faith Scale (PCFS) than did those who had been involved in ministry for five years or less. More specifically, they scored significantly higher ($p \leq .01$) in their participation in the practices of evangelism, giving financial support to their church, providing hospitality to strangers, volunteering time to help those less fortunate, promoting social justice, and discussing Christian responses to contemporary issues. The duration of participation or length of time volunteers are involved in community ministry activity shows a positive relationship with scores on the PCFS. See tables 1 and 2 at the end of this chapter. Other findings of this project can be found in Diana R. Garland, Dennis M. Myers, and Terry A. Wolfer, "Protestant Christian Volunteers in Community Social Service Programs: What Motivates, Challenges, and Sustains Them," *Administration in Social Work* 33, no. 1 (2009): 23–39; idem, "Social Work with Religious Volunteers: Activating and Sustaining Community Involvement," *Social Work* 53, no. 3 (2008): 255–65; Hugen, Wolfer, and Renkema, "Service and Faith"; and Myers, Wolfer, and Garland, "Congregational Service-Learning Characteristics."

6 See Jane Addams and Ruth W. Messinger, *Twenty Years at Hull-House* (New York: Macmillan, 1910); and Rosemary Skinner Keller, "Women Creating Communities—and Community—in the Name of the Social

Gospel," in *The Social Gospel Today*, ed. Christopher H. Evans (Louisville, Ky.: Westminster John Knox, 2001), 67–85.

7   Mary J. Oates, *The Catholic Philanthropic Tradition in America* (Bloomington: Indiana University Press, 1995).

8   T. Laine Scales, *"All That Fits a Woman": Training Southern Baptist Women for Charity and Mission, 1907–1926* (Macon, Ga.: Mercer University Press, 2000).

9   See Keller, "Women Creating Communities"; and Lois E. Myers, "'You Got Us All a-Pullin' Together': Southern Methodist Deaconesses in the Rural South, 1922–1940," in *Work, Family and Faith: Rural Southern Women in the Twentieth Century*, ed. Melissa Walker and Rebecca Sharpless (New York: Columbia University Press, 2006), 166–93.

10 For a history of the relationship between religious faith and social work, see the following works: Stacey Barker, "The Integration of Spirituality and Religion Content in Social Work Education: Where We've Been, Where We're Going," *Social Work & Christianity* 34, no. 2 (2008): 155–57; Ram Cnaan, Stephanie C. Boddie, and Rivka A. Danzig, "Teaching about Organized Religion in Social Work: Lessons and Challenges," in *Social Work and Divinity*, ed. Daniel B. Lee and Robert O'Gorman (Binghamton, N.Y.: The Haworth Pastoral Press, 2005), 93–110; David Derezotes, "Spirituality and Religiosity: Neglected Factors in Social Work Practice," *Arete* 20, no. 1 (1995): 1–15; Catherine Faver, "Religion, Research, and Social Work," *Social Thought* 3, no. 3 (1986): 19–29; Garland, "Church Social Work," in Hugen, *Christianity and Social Work*, 7–25; Diana Garland and Rick Chamiec-Case, "Before— and After—the Political Rhetoric: Faith-Based Child and Family Welfare Services," *Social Work & Christianity* 32, no. 1 (2005): 22–43; Ellen Netting, "Reflections on the Meaning of Sectarian, Religiously Affiliated, and Faith-Based Language: Implications for Human Service Consumers," *Social Work & Christianity* 29, no. 1 (2002): 13–30; and David Sherwood, "Integrating Christian Faith and Social Work: Reflections of a Social Work Educator," *Social Work & Christianity* 26, no. 1 (1999): 1–8.

11 For documentation of the social services congregations are providing, see the following: Ram Cnaan, "The Role of Religious Congregations in Providing Social Services" (paper presented at The Roundtable on Religion and Social Welfare Policy, Albany, N.Y., August 4, 2003); Ram Cnaan and Stephanie C. Boddie, "Charitable Choice and Faith-Based Welfare: A Call for Social Work," *Social Work* 47, no. 3 (2002): 224–35; Cnaan, Boddie, and Danzig, "Organized Religion in Social Work"; Ram Cnaan, et al., *The Invisible Caring Hand: American Congregations and the Provision of Welfare* (New York: New York University Press, 2002);

Ram Cnaan, Robert J. Wineburg, and Stephanie C. Boddie, *The Newer Deal: Social Work and Religion in Partnership* (New York: Columbia University Press, 1999); Amy Sherman, "Getting Down to Business: Models and First Steps for Christian Social Work," in Hugen and Scales, *Christianity and Social Work*, 291–304; Amy Sherman, *Reinvigorating Faith in Communities* (Fishers, Ind.: Hudson Institute, 2002); idem, *Restorers of Hope* (Wheaton: Crossway Books, 1997); idem, "Tracking Charitable Choice: A Study of the Collaboration between Faith-Based Organizations and the Government in Providing Social Services in Nine States," *Social Work & Christianity* 27, no. 2 (2000): 113–29.

12 Anne Farris, Richard P. Nathan, and David J. Wright, *The Expanding Administrative Presidency: George W. Bush and the Faith-Based Initiative* (Albany, N.Y.: The Roundtable on Religion and Social Welfare Policy, 2004), 5.

13 Garland, "Church Social Work," in Hugen, *Christianity and Social Work*, 7–25; Garland, et al., "Effective Leadership"; Dean Hoge, et al., "The Value of Volunteers as Resources for Congregations," *Journal for the Scientific Study of Religion* 37, no. 3 (1998): 470–80; Michael E. Sherr, *Social Work with Volunteers* (Chicago: Lyceum Press, 2008); Sherr and Hope Haslam Straughan, "Volunteerism, Social Work, and the Church: A Historic Overview and Look into the Future," *Social Work & Christianity* 32, no. 2 (2005): 97–115.

14 Dieter T. Hessel, *Social Ministry*, rev. ed.; Jon E. Singletary, "The Praxis of Social Work: A Model of How Faith Informs Practice Informs Faith," *Social Work & Christianity* 32, no. 1 (2005): 56–72.

15 Harvie Conn, *A Clarified Vision for Urban Mission: Dispelling Urban Stereotypes* (Grand Rapids: Zondervan, 1987).

16 Excellent introductions to this literature include the following: Dorothy C. Bass, "Keeping Sabbath," in Bass, *Practicing Our Faith*, 75–89; Bass and Dykstra, "Growing in the Practices of Faith"; Craig Dykstra, "Family Promises: Faith and Families in the Context of the Church," in Sawyers, *Faith and Families*, 137–63; idem, *Growing in the Life of Faith*; idem, "Reconceiving Practice"; idem, "What Is Faith?"; Dykstra and Bass, "Times of Yearning, Practices of Faith," in Bass, *Practicing Our Faith*, 1–12; Garland, *Sacred Stories*.

17 I first presented the concept of family faith practices in *Sacred Stories of Ordinary Families*.

18 Christine Pohl, *Making Room: Recovering Hospitality as a Christian Tradition* (Grand Rapids: Eerdmans, 1999).

Chapter 6

1 Rusaw and Swanson, *Extremely Focused Church*, 178.

2   Diana R. Garland, Terry A. Wolfer, and Dennis M. Myers, "How 35 Congregations Launched and Sustained Community Ministries," *Family and Community Ministries: Empowering through Faith* 35, no. 3 (2008): 229–57.

3   John Cosgrove, "Religious Congregations as Mediators of Devolution: A Study of Parish-Based Services," in *Social Work in an Era of Devolution: Toward a Just Practice*, ed. R. Perez-Koenig and B. Rock, 331–50 (New York: Fordham University Press, 2001).

4   Mark DeVries, *Family-based Youth Ministry* (Downers Grove, Ill.: InterVarsity, 2004).

5   For more on the concept of faith-families, see Garland, *Family Ministry*; idem, *Sacred Stories of Ordinary Families*; and idem, "'Who Is Your Family?'"

6   Bill Hybels, *The Volunteer Revolution: Unleashing the Power of Everybody* (Grand Rapids: Zondervan, 2004).

7   Hybels, *Volunteer Revolution*.

8   Roehlkepartain, Naftali, and Musegades, *Growing up Generous*, 116.

9   Rusaw and Swanson, *Externally Focused Church*, 181.

10 Sandy Sasso, "The Role of Narrative in the Spiritual Formation of Children: Walking in Cain's Shoes: Sacred Narrative with Question Marks," *Family Ministry: Empowering through Faith* 19, no. 2 (2005): 13–27.

11 This pastor taught me this culinary image.

12 Henri J. M. Nouwen, "The Path of Waiting," in *Finding My Way Home: Pathways to Life and the Spirit* (New York: Crossroad, 2001), 92–119.

13 Benson, Donahue, and Erickson, "Faith Maturity Scale." See above chapter 2, note 1.

14 The instruments are available from the author. The total list of items in the Christian Faith Practices Scale is found in table 1 of chapter 5. See also Bass, "Keeping Sabbath," in Bass, *Practicing Our Faith*, 75–89; and Bass and Dykstra, "Growing in the Practices of Faith," in Bass, *Practicing Our Faith*, 195–204.

15 For an academic presentation of these findings, see Garland, Myers, and Wolfer, "Social Work with Religious Volunteers," 255–65.

16 Wuthnow, *Learning to Care*.

17 Jim Dekker, "What Are We Doing with the Faith Development of Adolescents in Service Projects? A Response to Sherr, Garland, and Wolfer," *Journal of Youth Ministry* 6, no. 1 (2008): 55–65.

18 Daniel L. Buttry, "Surfacing and Analyzing Conflict: A Bible Study on the Ministry of Conflict Mediation," *Baptist Peacemaker* 17, no. 1 (1997): 10–11.

19 Some examples of ways congregations can tackle the causes of suffering

include Stan Hyland, "Building Neighborhoods, Not Just Houses," *Business Perspectives* 10, no. 2 (1997): 20–29; Kinney and Carver, "Urban Congregations as Incubators"; Nouwen, "Path of Waiting"; Michael Raschick, "Helping Working Poor Families with Low-Interest Loans," *Families in Society* 78, no. 1 (1997): 26–35; Michael M. O. Seipel, "Global Poverty: No Longer an Untouchable Problem," *International Social Work* 46, no. 2 (2003): 191–207; Phil Smith and Eric Thurman, *A Billion Bootstraps: Microcredit, Barefoot Banking, and the Business Solution for Ending Poverty* (New York: McGraw-Hill, 2007).

20 Davis, *Come, Go with Me*, 37.

21 Roehlkepartain, *Teaching Church*.

22 Introductions to Hessel's thought include Dieter T. Hessel, "Learning with the Justice-Active Church," in *Theological Education for Social Ministry*, ed. Dieter T. Hessel (New York: Pilgrim, 1988), 106–25; idem, *Social Ministry* (Philadelphia: Westminster Press, 1982), and the rev. ed. (1992); idem, *Theological Education*.

23 Ernest L. Boyer, "Creating the New American College," *Chronicle of Higher Education* (March 1994): A48; John Dewey, *Experience and Education* (New York: Collier Books, 1938).

24 Garland, *Sacred Stories*; David Sherwood, "Churches as Contexts for Social Work Practice: Connecting with the Mission and Identity of Congregations," *Social Work & Christianity* 30, no. 1 (2006): 1–13.

25 Rusaw and Swanson, *Externally Focused Church*, 193.

Bibliography

Abbott, S. Denise, Diana R. Garland, Alisa Huffman-Nevins, and Judy Boatwright Stewart. "Social Workers' Views of Local Churches as Service Providers: Impressions from an Exploratory Study." *Social Work & Christianity* 17 (1990): 7–16.

Addams, Jane, and Ruth W. Messinger. *Twenty Years at Hull-House*. New York: Macmillan, 1910.

Ammerman, Nancy T. *Pillars of Faith: American Congregations and Their Partners*. Berkeley: University of California Press, 2005.

Barker, Stacey L. "The Integration of Spirituality and Religion Content in Social Work Education: Where We've Been, Where We're Going." *Social Work & Christianity* 34, no. 2 (2008): 155–57.

Bass, Dorothy C. "Keeping Sabbath." In Bass, *Practicing Our Faith*, 75–89.

———, ed. *Practicing Our Faith: A Way of Life for a Searching People*. San Francisco: Jossey-Bass, 1997.

Bass, Dorothy C., and Craig Dykstra. "Growing in the Practices of Faith." In Bass, *Practicing Our Faith*, 195–204.

153

Benson, Peter L., Michael J. Donahue, and Joseph A. Erickson. "The Faith Maturity Scale: Conceptualization, Measurement, and Empirical Validation." *Research in the Social Scientific Study of Religion* 5 (1993): 1–26.

Billingsley, Andrew. *Mighty Like a River: The Black Church and Social Reform.* New York: Oxford University Press, 1999.

Boyer, Ernest L. "Creating the New American College." *Chronicle of Higher Education* (March 1994): A48.

Burgess, Ernest. "The Family as a Unity of Interacting Personalities." *The Family* 7, no. 1 (1926): 3–9.

Buttry, Daniel L. "Surfacing and Analyzing Conflict: A Bible Study on the Ministry of Conflict Mediation." *Baptist Peacemaker* 17, no. 1 (1997): 10–11.

Calhoun, Jack A. "Claiming Youth: A New Paradigm in Youth Policy." *New Directions for Philanthropic Fundraising* 38 (2002): 67–80.

Campbell, David E., and Steven J. Yonish. "Religion and Volunteering in America." In *Religion as Social Capital: Producing the Common Good,* edited by Corwin Smidt, 87–106. Waco, Tex.: Baylor University Press, 2003.

Charmaz, Kathy. *Constructing Grounded Theory: A Practical Guide through Qualitative Analysis.* London: Sage, 2006.

Chaves, Mark. *Congregations in America.* Cambridge, Mass.: Harvard University Press, 2004.

Cnaan, Ram A. "The Role of Religious Congregations in Providing Social Services." In *Roundtable on Religion and Social Welfare Policy.* Washington, D.C., 2003.

Cnaan, Ram A., and Stephanie C. Boddie. "Charitable Choice and Faith-Based Welfare: A Call for Social Work." *Social Work* 47, no. 3 (2002): 224–35.

Cnaan, Ram A., Stephanie C. Boddie, and Rivka A. Danzig. "Teaching about Organized Religion in Social Work: Lessons and Challenges." In *Social Work and Divinity,* edited by Daniel B. Lee and Robert O'Gorman, 93–110. Binghamton, N.Y.: Haworth Pastoral Press, 2005.

Cnaan, Ram A., Stephanie C. Boddie, Femida Handy, Gaynor Yancey, and Richard Schneider. *The Invisible Caring Hand: American Congregations and the Provision of Welfare*. New York: New York University Press, 2002.

Cnaan, Ram A., Robert J. Wineburg, and Stephanie C. Boddie. *The Newer Deal: Social Work and Religion in Partnership*. New York: Columbia University Press, 1999.

Coles, Robert. "The Profile of Spirituality of At-Risk Youth." In *The Ongoing Journey: Awakening Spiritual Life in At-Risk Youth*, edited by Terry Hyland and Ron Herron, 7–35. Boys Town, Neb.: Boys Town Press, 1995.

Conn, Harvie M. "Christian Social Ministry: What's the Problem?" *Urban Mission* 14, no. 1 (1996): 6–18.

———. *A Clarified Vision for Urban Mission: Dispelling Urban Stereotypes*. Grand Rapids: Zondervan, 1987.

Cosgrove, John. "Religious Congregations as Mediators of Devolution: A Study of Parish-Based Services." In *Social Work in an Era of Devolution: Toward a Just Practice*, edited by R. Perez-Koenig and B. Rock, 331–50. New York: Fordham University Press, 2001.

Crocker, David W. *Operation Inasmuch: Mobilizing Believers Beyond the Walls of the Church*. St. Louis, Mo.: Lake Hickory Resources, 2005.

Davis, C. Anne. *Come, Go with Me: Following Christ's Example of Ministry and Witness*. Birmingham, Ala.: Woman's Missionary Union, 1997.

Dekker, Jim. "What Are We Doing with the Faith Development of Adolescents in Service Projects? A Response to Sherr, Garland, and Wolfer." *The Journal of Youth Ministry* 6, no. 1 (2008): 55–65.

Derezotes, David S. "Spirituality and Religiosity: Neglected Factors in Social Work Practice." *Arete* 20, no. 1 (1995): 1–15.

DeVries, Mark. *Family-Based Youth Ministry*. Downers Grove, Ill.: InterVarsity, 2004.

Dewey, John. *Experience and Education*. New York: Collier Books, 1938.

Dudley, Carl S. *Basic Steps toward Community Ministry*. Washington, D.C.: Alban Institute, 1991.

———. *Next Steps in Community Ministry*. Washington, D.C.: The Alban Institute, 1996.

Dudley, Roger L. "Growing Faith." In *Valuegenesis: Faith in the Balance*, 57–80. Riverside, Calif.: La Sierra University Press, 1992.

Dykstra, Craig. "Family Promises: Faith and Families in the Context of the Church." In *Faith and Families*, edited by Lindell Sawyers, 137–63. Philadelphia: Geneva Press, 1986.

———. *Growing in the Life of Faith: Education and Christian Practices*. Louisville, Ky.: Geneva Press, 1999.

———. "Reconceiving Practice." In *Shifting Boundaries: Contextual Approaches to the Structure of Theological Education*, edited by Barbara Wheeler and Edward Farley, 37–55. Louisville, Ky.: Westminster John Knox, 1991.

———. "What Is Faith?: An Experiment in the Hypothetical Mode." In Dykstra and Parks, *Faith Development and Fowler*, 45–64.

Dykstra, Craig, and Dorothy C. Bass. "Times of Yearning, Practices of Faith." In Bass, *Practicing Our Faith*, 1–12.

Dykstra, Craig, and Sharon Parks, eds. *Faith Development and Fowler*. Birmingham, Ala.: Religious Education Press, 1986.

Farris, Anne, Richard P. Nathan, and David J. Wright. *The Expanding Administrative Presidency: George W. Bush and the Faith-Based Initiative*. Albany, N.Y.: The Roundtable on Religion and Social Welfare Policy, 2004.

Faver, Catherine A. "Religion, Research, and Social Work." *Social Thought* 3, no. 3 (1986): 19–29.

Fowler, James W. *Becoming Adult, Becoming Christian*. San Francisco: Jossey-Bass, 2000.

———. "Faith and the Structuring of Meaning." In Dykstra and Parks, *Faith Development and Fowler*, 15–42.

———. "Faith Development through the Family Life Cycle." In *Catholic Families: Growing and Sharing Faith*, 98–116. New Rochelle, N.Y.: Don Bosco Multimedia, 1990.

———. *Stages of Faith: The Psychology of Human Development and the Quest for Meaning*. San Francisco: Harper & Row, 1981.

———. *Weaving the New Creation: Stages of Faith and the Public Church.* San Francisco: Harper, 1991.

Gallagher, Nora. *Practicing Resurrection.* New York: Alfred A. Knopf, 2003.

Garland, David E., and Diana R. Garland. *Flawed Families of the Bible: How God Works through Imperfect Relationships.* Grand Rapids: Brazos Press, 2007.

Garland, Diana R. "The Church Census: A Congregational Assessment Tool for Family Ministry." *Family Ministry: Empowering through Faith* 18, no. 1 (2004): 46–61.

———. "Church Social Work." In *Christianity and Social Work: Readings on the Integration of Christian Faith and Social Work Practice,* edited by Beryl Hugen, 7–25. Botsford, Conn.: North American Association of Christians in Social Work, 1998.

———. "Faith Narratives of Congregants and Their Families." *Review of Religious Research* 44, no. 1 (2002): 68–91.

———. "Families and Their Faith." In Hugen and Scales, *Christianity and Social Work,* 119–43.

———. "The Families in Our Congregations: Initial Research Findings." *Family Ministry: Empowering through Faith* 18, no. 1 (2004): 62–87.

———. *Family Ministry: A Comprehensive Guide.* Grand Rapids: InterVarsity, 1999.

———. "Family Stories: Resources for Nurturing Family Faith in Congregational Life." *Family Ministry: Empowering through Faith* 18, no. 3 (2004): 26–44.

———. "The Sacred in Family Stories." *Family Ministry: Empowering through Faith* 19, no. 2 (2005): 41–60.

———. *Sacred Stories of Ordinary Families: Living the Faith in Daily Life.* San Francisco: Jossey-Bass, 2003.

———. "'Who Is Your Family?' Membership Composition of American Protestant Families." *Social Work & Christianity* 29, no. 3 (2002): 183–223.

Garland, Diana R., and Jo A. Edmonds. "Family Life of Baptists." *Family Ministry: Empowering through Faith* 21, no. 1 (2007): 6–21.

Garland, Diana R., and Rick Chamiec-Case. "Before—and after—the Political Rhetoric: Faith-Based Child and Family Welfare Services." *Social Work & Christianity* 29, no. 1 (2005): 223–43.

Garland, Diana R., Beryl Hugen, Dennis Myers, Paula Sheridan, David Sherwood, and Terry A. Wolfer. "Effective Leadership of Faith-Motivated Volunteers in Community Service Programs." Paper presented at the Annual Program Meeting of the Council on Social Work Education, Nashville, Tenn., February 2002.

Garland, Diana R., Dennis M. Myers, and Terry A. Wolfer. "The Impact of Volunteering on Christian Faith and Congregational Life: The Service and Faith Project." Baylor University. http://www.baylor.edu/~CFCM/.

————. "Learning to See People as God Sees Them: Outcomes of Community Service for Congregational Volunteers." *Review of Religious Research* (forthcoming).

————. "Protestant Christian Volunteers in Community Social Service Programs: What Motivates, Challenges, and Sustains Them." *Administration in Social Work* 33, no. 1 (2009): 23–39.

————. "Social Work with Religious Volunteers: Activating and Sustaining Community Involvement." *Social Work* 53, no. 3 (2008): 255–65.

Garland, Diana R., Terry A. Wolfer, and Dennis M. Myers. "How 35 Congregations Launched and Sustained Community Ministries." *Family and Community Ministries: Empowering through Faith* 35, no. 3 (2008): 229–57.

Garland, Diana R., and Pamela Yankeelov. "The Church Census." *Family Ministry: Empowering through Faith* 12, no. 3 (1998): 11–22.

————. "The Strengths, Stresses and Faith Practices of Congregational Families." *Family Ministry: Empowering through Faith* 15, no. 3 (2001): 28–47.

Hall, Kenneth L. *Inside Outside: The Church in Social Ministry.* Dallas: Family Matters Ministry of the Buckner Foundation, 1997.

Hessel, Dieter T. "Learning with the Justice-Active Church." In *Theological Education for Social Ministry*, edited by Dieter T. Hessel, 106–25. New York: Pilgrim, 1988.

———. *Social Ministry.* Philadelphia: Westminster, 1982.

———. *Social Ministry.* Revised ed. Philadelphia: Westminster, 1992.

———, ed. *Theological Education for Social Ministry.* New York: Pilgrim, 1988.

Hoge, Dean R., Charles Zech, Patrick McNamara, and Michael J. Donahue. "The Value of Volunteers as Resources for Congregations." *Journal for the Scientific Study of Religion* 37, no. 3 (1998): 470–80.

Hugen, Beryl, and T. Laine Scales, eds. *Christianity and Social Work: Readings on the Integration of Faith and Social Work Practice.* Botsford, Conn.: North American Association of Christians in Social Work, 2002.

Hugen, Beryl, Terry A. Wolfer, and Jennifer Ubels Renkema. "Service and Faith: The Impact on Faith of Community Ministry Participation." *Review of Religious Research* 47, no. 4 (2006): 409–26.

Hybels, Bill. *The Volunteer Revolution: Unleashing the Power of Everybody.* Grand Rapids: Zondervan, 2004.

Hyland, Stan. "Building Neighborhoods, Not Just Houses." *Business Perspectives* 10, no. 2 (1997): 20–29.

Johnson, Luke Timothy. *The Acts of the Apostles.* Edited by Daniel J. Harrington, Sacra Pagina. Collegeville, Minn.: The Liturgical Press, 1992.

Keller, Rosemary Skinner. "Women Creating Communities—and Community—in the Name of the Social Gospel." In *The Social Gospel Today*, edited by Christopher H. Evans, 67–85. Louisville, Ky.: Westminster John Knox, 2001.

Kinney, Nancy T., and Mary L. Carver. "Urban Congregations as Incubators of Service Organizations." In *34th Annual Conference of the Association for Research on Nonprofit Organizations and Voluntary Action (ARNOVA).* Washington, D.C., 2005.

McBride, Joseph. *Stephen Spielberg: A Biography.* New York: Simon & Schuster, 1997.

McCubbin, H. I., and C. Figley, eds. *Stress and the Family.* Vol. 1, *Coping with Transitions.* New York: Brunner/Mazel, 1983.

McCubbin, Hamilton I., and Charles R. Figley. "Bridging Normative and Catastrophic Family Stress." In McCubbin and Figley, *Stress and the Family.* Vol. 1, *Coping with Transitions.*

McCubbin, Hamilton I., and Marilyn A. McCubbin. "Resilient Families, Competencies, Supports, and Coping over the Life Cycle." In *Faith and Families*, edited by Lindell Sawyers, 65–88. Philadelphia: The Geneva Press, 1986.

McCubbin, H. I., M. A. McCubbin, and A. I. Thompson. "Resiliency in Families: The Role of Family Schema and Appraisal in Family Adaptation to Crises." In *Family Relations: Challenges for the Future*, edited by T. H. Brubaker, 154. Newbury Park: Sage, 1993.

McElway, Alexander J. "The Systematic Theology of Faith: A Protestant Perspective." In *Handbook of Faith*, edited by James Michael Lee, 164–200. Birmingham, Ala.: Religious Education Press, 1990.

Meilaender, Gilbert. "A Christian View of the Family." In *Rebuilding the Nest: A New Commitment to the American Family*, edited by David Blankenhorn, Steven Bayme, and Jean Bethke Elshtain, 133–47. Milwaukee: Family Service America, 1990.

Myers, Dennis R, Terry A. Wolfer, and Diana R. Garland. "Congregational Service-Learning Characteristics and Volunteer Faith Development." *Religious Education* 103, no. 3 (2008): 369–86.

Myers, Lois E. "'You Got Us All a-Pullin' Together': Southern Methodist Deaconesses in the Rural South, 1922–1940." In *Work, Family and Faith: Rural Southern Women in the Twentieth Century*, edited by Melissa Walker and Rebecca Sharpless, 166–93. New York: Columbia University Press, 2006.

Nelson, M. C. "Why Do They Do It? A Study of Volunteer Commitment in the Parish Setting." *The Journal of Volunteer Administration* 17, no. 2 (1999): 30–37.

Netting, F. Ellen. "Reflections on the Meaning of Sectarian, Religiously-Affiliated, and Faith-Based Language: Implications for Human Service Consumers." *Social Work & Christianity* 29, no. 1 (2002): 13–30.

Nouwen, Henri J. M. "The Path of Waiting." In *Finding My Way Home: Pathways to Life and the Spirit*, 92–119. New York: Crossroad, 2001.

Oates, Mary J. *The Catholic Philanthropic Tradition in America.* Bloomington: Indiana University Press, 1995.

Piedmont, R. L., and R. Nelson. "A Psychometric Evaluation of the Short Form of the Faith Maturity Scale." *Social Scientific Study of Religion* 12 (2001): 165–83.

Pohl, Christine D. *Making Room: Recovering Hospitality as a Christian Tradition.* Grand Rapids: Eerdmans, 1999.

Raschick, Michael. "Helping Working Poor Families with Low-Interest Loans." *Families in Society* 78, no. 1 (1997): 26–35.

Roehlkepartain, Eugene C. *The Teaching Church: Moving Christian Education to Center Stage.* Nashville: Abingdon, 1993.

———. "What Makes Faith Mature?" *The Christian Century* 107, no. 6 (1990): 496–99.

Roehlkepartain, Eugene C., Elanah Dalyah Naftali, and Laura Musegades. *Growing up Generous: Engaging Youth in Giving and Serving.* Bethesda, Md.: Alban Institute, 2000.

Roehlkepartain, Eugene C., and Dorothy L. Williams. *Exploring Faith Maturity.* Minneapolis: Lutheran Brotherhood, 1990.

Rusaw, Rick, and Eric Swanson. *The Externally Focused Church.* Loveland, Colo.: Group, 2004.

Sasso, Sandy. "The Role of Narrative in the Spiritual Formation of Children: Walking in Cain's Shoes: Sacred Narrative with Question Marks." *Family Ministry: Empowering through Faith* 19, no. 2 (2005): 13–27.

Sawicki, Marianne. "Recognizing the Risen Lord." *Theology Today* 44, no. 4 (1988): 441–49.

Scales, T. Laine. *"All That Fits a Woman": Training Southern Baptist Women for Charity and Mission, 1907–1926.* Macon, Ga.: Mercer University Press, 2000.

Seipel, Michael M. O. "Global Poverty: No Longer an Untouchable Problem." *International Social Work* 46, no. 2 (2003): 191–207.

Sherman, Amy. "Getting Down to Business: Models and First Steps for Christian Social Work." In Hugan and Scales, *Christianity and Social Work,* 291–304.

———. *Reinvigorating Faith in Communities.* Fishers, Ind.: Hudson Institute, 2002.

————. *Restorers of Hope.* Wheaton: Crossway Books, 1997.

————. "Tracking Charitable Choice: A Study of the Collaboration between Faith-Based Organizations and the Government in Providing Social Services in Nine States." *Social Work & Christianity* 27, no. 2 (2000): 113–29.

Sherr, Michael E. *Social Work with Volunteers.* Chicago: Lyceum, 2008.

Sherr, Michael E., Diana Garland, and Terry Wolfer. "The Role of Community Service in the Faith Development of Adolescents." *Journal of Youth Ministry* 6, no. 1 (2007): 43–54.

Sherr, Michael E., and Hope Haslam Straughan. "Volunteerism, Social Work, and the Church: A Historic Overview and Look into the Future." *Social Work & Christianity* 32, no. 2 (2005): 97–115.

Sherr, Michael, James Stamey, and Diana R. Garland. "Empowering Faith Practices: A Validation Study of the Christian Faith Practices Scale." *Journal of Family and Community Ministries* 23, no. 1 (2009): 27–35.

Sherwood, David A. "Churches as Contexts for Social Work Practice: Connecting with the Mission and Identity of Congregations." *Social Work & Christianity* 30, no. 1 (2006): 1–13.

————. "Integrating Christian Faith and Social Work: Reflections of a Social Work Educator." *Social Work & Christianity* 26, no. 1 (1999): 1–8.

Singletary, Jon E. "The Praxis of Social Work: A Model of How Faith Informs Practice Informs Faith." *Social Work & Christianity* 32, no. 1 (2005): 56–72.

Smith, Christian, and Melinda Lundquist Denton. *Soul Searching: The Religious and Spiritual Lives of American Teenagers.* New York: Oxford University Press, 2005.

Smith, Phil, and Eric Thurman. *A Billion Bootstraps: Microcredit, Barefoot Banking, and the Business Solution for Ending Poverty.* New York: McGraw-Hill, 2007.

Strauss, Anselm, and Juliet Corbin. *Basics of Qualitative Research: Techniques and Procedures for Developing Grounded Theory.* 2nd ed. Thousand Oaks, Calif.: Sage, 1998.

Unruh, Heidi Rolland. "Mobilizing and Equipping Your Church for Holistic Ministry." Paper presented at Conference on Working Toegether to Serve the Needy: Welfare Reform and the Faith Community in Greater Philadelphia, Philadelphia, Penn., December 8, 1998.

Watkins, Derrell E. *Christian Social Ministry: An Introduction.* Nashville: Broadman & Holman, 1994.

Weiss, Robert S. *Learning from Strangers: The Art and Method of Qualitative Interview Studies.* New York: Free Press, 1994.

Wuthnow, Robert. *Acts of Compassion: Caring for Others and Helping Ourselves.* Princeton: Princeton University Press, 1991.

———. *Learning to Care: Elementary Kindness in an Age of Indifference.* Princeton: Princeton University Press, 1995.

Index